Janet DeCaster Perrin

DOG tales & pup PARABLES

31 Devotions for a Dog Lover's Heart

BroadStreet
PUBLISHING

BroadStreet Publishing Group, LLC
Racine, Wisconsin, USA
BroadStreetPublishing.com

DOG Tales & pup PARABLES: 31 Devotions for a Dog Lover's Heart

Copyright © 2016 Janet DeCaster Perrin

ISBN-13: 978-1-4245-5263-4 (hardcover)
ISBN-13: 978-1-4245-5264-1 (e-book)

Stock or custom editions of BroadStreet Publishing titles may be purchased in bulk for educational, business, ministry, fundraising, or sales promotional use. For information, please e-mail info@broadstreetpublishing.com.

Art direction by Chris Garborg, garborgdesign.com
Typesetting by Katherine Lloyd, theDESKonline.com

Printed in China
16 17 18 19 20 5 4 3 2 1

Contents

Introduction

~~🦴~~

Most dog owners know the unconditional love of their faithful pet. No matter what kind of day we've had or how our own behavior may not have measured up on any given day, there's Fido or Spot with a wagging tail and happy eyes. On more than one occasion, my dogs have cheered me up when no one else can.

I love God and have put my faith and trust in Jesus Christ, His Son. I like to think that God has sent my dogs as a tiny representation of His unconditional love for me. Though they can be a lot of work and try my patience (and the patience of my family), my dogs have brought a smile to my face through the years. When I think of the depths of world poverty, it truly is a luxury of a very few to own an animal that is not being raised for food or for a specific job, such as shepherding sheep. On a recent missions trip to the Dominican Republic, I noticed many sick stray dogs wandering the streets. Some were so overtaken with mange that I was heartbroken just looking at them. I also saw dogs shepherding cows along the beach. None of these dogs were the friendly, sleek, suburban American pets to which I am accustomed. Of course, we were there to minister to the people, but the dogs caught my attention too. So it's with a heart of thanks to God for the privilege of dog ownership that I share these testimonies of how God has used experiences with my dogs as illustrations of His kingdom principles.

Do my dogs speak to me? Certainly not! If my dogs suddenly spoke English out loud (like Mr. Ed, the talking horse on the 1960s American TV show), I'd be in big trouble, not only psychologically, but biblically speaking. For proof, see the story of Balaam and his donkey found in the Old Testament of the Holy Bible (Numbers 22:22–35). My dogs don't speak, but God does. Let me explain. My dog-walking time is often also my prayer time. As I walk and pray, the Holy Spirit uses simple illustrations from my dogs' lives, behavior, or training to communicate with me and emphasize points He has been trying to get across in other ways. As I pray, the Holy Spirit gives me impressions that provide directions and answers to my prayers in simple ways I can understand. As I've walked more and more closely with Jesus Christ, I've learned to follow His lead. Let me tell you how my journey with Him began.

My Personal Faith Testimony

Before you begin reading, I would like to share my personal faith testimony. I hope it will encourage you in your faith journey and give you some perspective on my writing.

I grew up singing, "Jesus loves me, this I know, for the

Bible tells me so," in Sunday school at our church. I am afraid, however, that I repeated those words without really knowing in my heart they were true. I had a longing to know the love that I sang about. However, we didn't read the Bible at home, and no one ever seemed to tell me what those words meant. I would sit in Sunday school wondering if the Bible stories I heard were any different than the fairy tales we read or the cartoons I watched on television at home. I am sure my Sunday school teachers, my parents, and others tried to convey the truth of God's love to me, but somehow I missed it. I always wondered about the truth of the gospel I heard as a child, but I wasn't absolutely sure.

It wasn't until after a very near brush with death through a serious sickness as an adult that I realized those Bible stories and the words of that Sunday school song were true. Here is how I came to believe that Jesus Christ is the Son of God and put my trust in Him.

One evening I was lying in my bed reading the Bible. I had finally decided to read the Bible because I had been gravely ill and I had a brother who was about to have a serious surgery. Desperate circumstances have a way of reminding us of what is really important in life. That particular night, I felt a deep longing to pray for my brother's protection and healing. However, despite a nearly lifelong habit of church attendance, I realized that I didn't know how to pray, and I didn't really know the one to whom I was praying. So I grabbed the Bible off our bedroom bookshelf and flipped it open. It was the

Bible that my mother had given me ten years earlier as a wedding gift. That night, I read these words Jesus spoke in John 14:6: "I am the Way—yes, and the Truth and the Life. No one can get to the Father except by means of me" (TLB). It felt as if those words came to life, leapt off that Bible page, and touched my heart. I had a sudden, instantaneous understanding that the Bible was true. In that moment a love and peace I had never known flooded through me.

After years of attending churches as a matter of religious habit, I suddenly knew, in my own heart, Jesus Christ's forgiveness and love. The backstory of my years of wandering in the wilderness, apart from God's love and Christ's forgiveness, would take too long to share here. Suffice it to say that, in an instant, a then-thirty-six-year-old wife and stay-at-home mom was radically converted to Christ. I fell deeply in love with Jesus, and He began to become my Lord.

I came to know Jesus more and more through reading His Word, spending quiet time with Him, and enjoying fellowship with other believers. He began to heal the broken places within my soul. That healing wasn't instantaneous, as my conversion had been. Rather, it is an ongoing process called *sanctification*. In Luke 4:18–19, Jesus proclaimed Himself to be the Messiah that Isaiah had prophesied. He said,

> "The Spirit of the LORD is upon Me, because He has anointed Me to preach the gospel to the poor; He has sent Me to heal the brokenhearted, to proclaim liberty

to the captives and recovery of sight to the blind, to set at liberty those who are oppressed; to proclaim the acceptable year of the LORD."

Jesus said He was the one who heals broken hearts and breaks bondages. I can testify to the truth of those statements, through personal experience. Day by day, week by week, year by year, through the power of His beautiful Holy Spirit, Jesus began to change me and mend my broken heart, broken thinking, broken self-image, and broken behavior.

I attended a small local Bible college part time when my daughters were in preschool and elementary school. Later I became a part-time staff pastor at a local church and then I taught as an adjunct at the same Bible college I had attended. While I was sharing God's love with others, the Holy Spirit was changing me and mending the broken places in my life. It is sometimes a slow, painful process to be healed of the wounds that sin has made in your heart. My thought life, in particular, needed a lot of His love to overcome wrong thinking patterns about my relationships, others, and myself. I am still a work in progress, but I find that if I daily seek God's help through reading His Word and praying, He is always there for me. He is as close as a prayer.

Using This Devotional

In the New Testament of the Holy Bible, Jesus Christ used simple stories from everyday life, called parables, to demonstrate spiritual truths. For examples, see the parable of the sower and the explanation of parables found in Matthew 13 or the parable of the persistent widow told by Jesus in Luke 18. It is my hope that through the testimonies of my own experiences with my dogs and my friends' dogs, which the Holy Spirit has used to illuminate His truth in my heart, He will also speak to your heart.

Focus Bible verses and prayers of faith (declarative prayers and prayers of thanksgiving based upon Bible verses) are included as faith builders. According to Ephesians 6, the Word of God is like a sword to be used in spiritual battle. Hebrews 4:12 states, "The word of God is living and powerful and sharper than any two-edged sword, piercing even to the division of soul and spirit, and of joints and marrow, and is a discerner of the thoughts and intents of the heart." Memorizing and praying God's Word will help you change bad habits, conquer sinful attitudes, and overcome difficulties in your life. Devotional thoughts for journaling are included for those readers who like to journal and process spiritual truth through writing.

May God's unconditional love (which is far, far greater than your dog's love!) touch you as you read these *Dog Tales & Pup Parables* testimonies, memorize His Word, and pray the included prayers of faith to strengthen your Christian walk. Be blessed!

Your dog-loving friend in Jesus Christ,
Janet DeCaster Perrin

1

THE SOCK PROBLEM

A Lesson in God's Love

For God so loved the world that He gave His only begotten Son, that whoever believes in Him should not perish but have everlasting life. For God did not send His Son into the world to condemn the world, but that the world through Him might be saved. (John 3:16–17)

A trail of socks went up our stairs. Exasperated, I knew that Joy, our Bichon-Cavalier mix (Cavachon) puppy, then probably less than a year old, had stolen more of our socks. She had a real penchant for chewing on socks and raiding the bathroom garbage cans. I always knew when someone hadn't thrown their laundry in the basket. I'd find a sock in some strange place or catch Joy in the act with a sock in her mouth. It was frustrating because we lost a lot of good socks that way.

On Mondays, the church where I worked part time as

a staff pastor was closed. It was the perfect day to clean the house and get our household organized for the week while the kids were at school. I am a multitasking mom. While I cleaned the house and performed other mundane tasks, I prayed. I was also thinking about the sermon I was going to share at our Sunday night church service later that week on the love of God. As I prayed and cleaned the house, once again, I caught Joy with one of my favorite bright pink thermal socks in her mouth. When you live in Minnesota, you learn to value thermal socks during the long, cold winters.

As I came up the stairs and saw Joy happily chewing on my beloved sock, I was mad at her. She ran and hid under our bed. She was so small. I had no way to get her or the sock out because she hid just beyond my reach. In the midst of my consternation with Joy, the Holy Spirit broke through my thoughts and spoke in the quiet of my heart. He simply said, *I love you in spite of your sock problems.* The still, small voice of the Holy Spirit brought His sweet peace into my heart. God was telling me He loves me even when I don't measure up or I fail Him in some way! He loves me, just as I loved our little dog. You see, even though I sometimes found Joy's sock-stealing ways inconvenient, I always loved her. She made me laugh and smile and also laugh at myself. She was a source of joy to my kids and myself. When any of us felt blue, Joy, a born-and-bred lap dog, would come sit with us and everything would be okay. When we were petting Joy, we'd feel much better.

When the Holy Spirit whispered His love for me, *despite my sock problems*, I knew exactly what He meant. I knew He loved me and that I made Him smile, despite the fact that I sometimes messed up. His words deeply impressed in me that His love for me was unconditional. In other words, His love didn't depend upon my performance. This fresh revelation of His love gave me the perfect sermon illustration! I ran to get my camera and took a photo of Joy with my bright pink thermal sock in her mouth. My day of prayer and housecleaning brightened immeasurably, and I had peace about my sermon message that week. That Sunday evening, I displayed the photo on the screens in the church sanctuary when I was teaching.

I believe God wanted to tell not only me, but also you, that He loves you despite your "sock problems." Let me explain. God is well aware of your shortcomings. They are no surprise to Him. As Paul wrote in Romans 3:23, "All have sinned and fall short of the glory of God." Remember that "God so loved the world [that includes you and me] that He gave His only begotten Son, that whoever believes in Him should not perish but have everlasting life. For God did not send His Son into the world to condemn the world, but that the world through Him might be saved" (John 3:16–17). God's love is unconditional. When you believe in and receive Jesus Christ as your Savior, God sees you and all of your sin through the sacrifice of His Son's blood. Perfectly cleansed, perfectly forgiven, perfectly loved. He loves you, and He loves me, despite the fact that we are still imperfect. Receive His love today and let His love wash over you. With sure confidence in His love for you, you can be empowered to serve Him and to love others in His name. I love my little dog, even when she steals my socks. Remember that God loves you, too, despite your "sock problems."

Personal Prayer

Lord, I confess that I have sinned against you in many ways. Please forgive me. Help me to understand the greatness of your love, which overcomes my fears and failures. I love you. Thank you that you love me, too, just the way I am. Amen.

Focus Verses and Prayers of Faith

John 3:16–17 For God so loved the world that He gave His only begotten Son, that whoever believes in Him should not perish but have everlasting life. For God did not send His Son into the world to condemn the world, but that the world through Him might be saved. · *Father, I thank you that you love me so much that you sent Jesus Christ to save me.*

Proverbs 8:17 I love those who love me, and those who seek me diligently will find me. · *As I diligently seek you, Lord, I will find you.*

Romans 5:5 Now hope does not disappoint, because the love of God has been poured out in our hearts by the Holy Spirit who was given to us. · *The love of God has been poured into my heart by the Holy Spirit.*

Ephesians 3:17–21 That Christ may dwell in your hearts through faith; that you, being rooted and grounded in love, may be able to comprehend with all the saints what is the width and length and depth and height—to know the love of Christ which passes knowledge; that you may be filled with all the fullness of God. Now to Him who is able to do exceedingly abundantly above all that we ask or think, according to the power that works in us, to Him be glory in the church by Christ Jesus to all generations, forever and ever. Amen. · *Father, I thank you that Christ dwells in my heart by faith, that I am rooted and grounded in the love of Christ, and that along with all the saints I am able to comprehend the width and length and depth and height of the love of God.*

Devotional Thoughts for Personal Journaling

1. Do you really understand the depth of God's love for you? Spend the next few days reading and meditating on the above Bible verses and others related to God's love. Spend time writing about God's love for you and ask His Holy Spirit for a fresh revelation of that love.

2. Ask the Holy Spirit which areas of your life are like Joy's sock problems: repeated areas of weakness and failure. Pray and journal about the following:

- How can you gain the victory over that weakness from a position of security and assurance of God's love?
- How can you begin to know and understand the love of God more and more to be free from any condemning or shame-filled thoughts that the enemy tries to bring as a result of that weakness?
- Pray and journal a plan to gain the victory in this area of your life, both to know His love and to overcome the problem from that place of love.

2

THE LITTLE DOG UNDER THE TABLE

A Lesson in Persistent Prayer

Then Jesus…departed to the region of Tyre and Sidon…. A woman…cried out to Him, saying, "Have mercy on me, O Lord, Son of David! My daughter is severely demon-possessed." But He answered her not a word…. Then she came and worshiped Him, saying, "Lord, help me!" But He answered and said, "It is not good to take the children's bread and throw it to the little dogs." And she said, "Yes, Lord, yet even the little dogs eat the crumbs which fall from their masters' table." Then Jesus answered and said to her, "O woman, great is your faith! Let it be to you as you desire." And her daughter was healed from that very hour. (Matthew 15:21–28)

By the time our dog Joy was two years old, she had become an expert in waiting for food to drop from the table while we were eating or off the counter while I was preparing a meal. She wasn't always quick to respond to the command, "Come." But whenever food fell, one of us would say, "Joy, come and clean up the floor," and into the kitchen she'd run. I began to feel that Joy was really earning her keep as she was saving me so much time on sweeping and mopping. She was too short to actually reach the table, but she was great at waiting for crumbs to drop. And she was diligent and persistent in her task. Whenever I was in the kitchen, Joy would circle the center island or sit under the table, waiting for the inevitable crumb to drop.

Not only was Joy an expert crumb catcher but she also camped out next to the food bin and just stared at me when it was time for her breakfast or dinner. Likewise, if Joy was upstairs at night without her water bowl, she simply walked into the master bathroom, sat down near the sink, and stared at us until we got the unspoken message, *Get me a drink!* One of us then obediently filled a Dixie cup for Joy's bedtime drink. She became a great communicator. She fully expected, and still expects, that her masters will meet her needs. She patiently waits for me (or another family member) to do so.

As I was preparing to speak at our church one week on the subject of divine healing prayer, I began to contemplate Matthew 15:21–28. In that passage, Jesus had just come from another contentious encounter with the Jewish Pharisees (religious leaders who followed many religious traditions but lacked faith in God). They had accused Jesus' disciples of failing to adhere to all of the religious laws. In that context, Jesus (himself a Jewish teacher) encountered a Gentile (non-Jewish) woman. She cried out to Him, "Have mercy on me, O Lord, Son of David! My daughter is severely demon-possessed" (v. 22). She clearly recognized Jesus' messianic authority and power, in stark contrast to Matthew's description of the Pharisees' doubt-filled ridicule and scorn. This woman recognized that Jesus had the power to deliver her daughter from the demon possession that gripped her. Jesus replied that He was sent to the Jews only, declaring, "It is not good to take the children's [Jews'] bread and give it to the little dogs" (v. 26). The Gentile woman, however, refused to give up. She had faith that Jesus could heal her daughter. She did not walk away dejected after hearing Jesus say no, essentially, in response to her request. Instead, she replied, "Yes, Lord, yet even the little dogs eat the crumbs which fall from their master's table" (v. 27). Jesus, perhaps surprised at her persistence and faith, said, "O woman, great is your faith! Let it be to you as you desire." Then the text states, "And her daughter was healed from that very hour" (v. 28). The Gentile woman received healing for her demon-possessed child because she didn't take no for an answer. She had faith that Jesus could heal and, despite her ethnic disadvantage and the initial no she received to her request, she persisted. Jesus rewarded her persistent faith and declaration of truth.

As I studied that passage, it reminded me of Jesus' instruction on prayer in Luke 18 using the parable of the persistent widow. In that passage, Jesus commended a wronged widow for going continually before an unjust judge for justice. She received her justice in the end because of her stubborn, continual pursuit of an answer. Speaking to believers and exhorting them to be like the widow in the parable, Jesus said in Luke 18:7, "And shall God not avenge His own elect who cry out day and night to Him, though He bears long with them?" In other words, Jesus was saying, *Don't give up when going to God in prayer.* The Gentile woman was so humble that she compared herself to a little dog under a table, waiting for the master's crumbs to fall. Likewise, the persistent widow in Jesus' parable wouldn't stop going to the judge until her request was granted. By using the story of the Gentile woman and the parable of the persistent widow, Jesus clearly instructs believers to persist in prayer.

Our dog Joy knows that good things come from her masters' table (and sink). She also knows how to wait until those crumbs fall. With all her persistence and seeking for crumbs, Joy became my sermon illustration that week. This time, the photo I put up on the big screens in the church sanctuary was of Joy waiting patiently under our kitchen table while we ate. I think she got the point across to my audience.

How about you? When your prayers aren't answered right away, do you quit and give up in discouragement? Don't give up! Don't quit! Be like that Gentile woman who wouldn't take no for an answer. She knew that good things came from the Master's hand. My dog Joy knows that too.

Personal Prayer

Lord, help me to humble myself like the Gentile woman and to persevere in prayer like the persistent widow. Give me patience and persistence to wait upon your good answers to my prayers, according to your will. Amen.

Focus Verses and Prayers of Faith

Luke 18:1–8

Then He spoke a parable to them, that men always ought to pray and not lose heart, saying: "There was in a certain city a judge who did not fear God nor regard man. Now there was a widow in that city; and she came to him, saying, 'Get justice for me from my adversary.' And he would not for a while; but afterward he said within himself, 'Though I do not fear God nor regard man, yet because this widow troubles me I will avenge her, lest by her continual coming she weary me.'" Then the Lord said, "Hear what the unjust judge said. And shall God not avenge His own elect who cry out day and night to Him, though He bears long with them? I tell you that He will avenge them speedily. Nevertheless, when the Son of Man comes, will He really find faith on the earth?" · *I will pray continually and not lose heart, and my God will avenge me because I cry out to him day and night by faith.*

Matthew 7:7–8 "Ask, and it will be given to you; seek, and you will find; knock, and it will be opened to you. For everyone who asks receives, and he who seeks finds, and to him who knocks it will be opened." • *I will ask, seek, and knock after your will, God, and you will make it known to me. I will continually pray with persistence by your Spirit, and you will answer me according to your will.*

Devotional Thoughts for Personal Journaling

1. Recall a time when a long-term, persistent prayer was answered. Journal your memory of the waiting time and the end result. What did you learn in the process? How did that situation change you? Praise God for His answer!

2. Ask the Holy Spirit to reveal any areas of impatience in your life. Over the next several days or weeks, begin to ask Him for the faith to wait for His answer and persist in prayer even during a long delay. Have you noticed any changes in your heart since you began to pray?

3. Study the life of Abraham and Sarah in Genesis 15–21 over several days or weeks. Pay particular attention to the time of God's promise to Abraham and the timing of the fulfillment of that promise. Read in conjunction with Hebrews 11:8–11. Journal your reflections on Abraham and Sarah's long-awaited answer. What does this teach you about the importance of persistent prayer and believing in those things you do not see?

3

A GENTLE LEADER

A Lesson in the Holy Spirit's Guidance

The Lord is my shepherd; I shall not want. He makes me to lie
down in green pastures; He leads me beside the still waters.
He restores my soul; He leads me in the paths of righteousness for His name's sake. (Psalm 23:1–3)

I had been frustrated trying to teach our new puppy, Kona, a
three-month-old Portuguese Water Dog, to walk on a leash.
She was afraid to leave our property and would refuse to
walk out of the driveway. Every day I would carry her across
the cul-de-sac and down to the walking path, out of view of
our home, for a walk. With her growing legs and increasing
weight, this was a challenge. We would get to the walking
trail that ran through our neighborhood, and down Kona
would sit. She would just sit, stare, and whimper, refusing
to move. Coaxing her helped a little at first. Eventually she'd

walk. However, after a couple of weeks of this routine, I was becoming frustrated with her. My impatience with our little puppy was growing. In exasperation, there were times when I would practically drag the poor little thing behind me down the street, feeling twinges of guilt along with impatience. Poor Kona!

In the midst of this frustrating scenario one day, the Holy Spirit interrupted my thoughts. In His still, small voice, in the quiet of my heart, He said, *Don't pull her, gently lead her. I don't pull you, I gently lead you.* I was convicted in my heart of my own impatience with our dear little puppy. Proverbs 12:10 says, "The godly care for their animals, but the wicked are always cruel" (NLT). I had memorized that proverb, and it came to my mind at that moment. I felt terrible about practically dragging my pup down the road. I repented and asked for God's help to train the puppy. I also asked for grace and patience for her. I began to speak to her sweetly, bringing treats with me when we walked. I got some great pointers at a puppy class we began attending at the local pet store, and things started to improve. The beginnings of our walks were still challenging, however. So I asked the Lord to help and guide me. Again, the Holy Spirit reminded me to *gently lead* my puppy, as He had begun to gently lead me when I was young in Christ. How could I possibly resist that loving admonition from the Lord? I couldn't. His kindness was leading me to repentance.

After I received that impression from the Holy Spirit, I

also remembered there is a dog-training tool called the Gentle Leader®. It's a type of mouth-and-head harness that helps an owner walk her dog without pulling on his neck. The next day I went to our puppy class, and the teacher wholeheartedly recommended a Gentle Leader. With my increased patience and the Gentle Leader, our walks became a pleasure to both Kona and me. Also, I'm sure our older dog Joy began to appreciate a more peaceful walk.

The guidance of the Holy Spirit is clearly explained in Scripture. Recall that Christian doctrine teaches that God is eternally existent in three distinct but unified persons: the Father, the Son (Jesus Christ), and the Holy Spirit. In the Old Testament, in Psalm 23:1–3, God is described as a shepherd who leads. In the New Testament, Jesus says in John 10:3–4, "He calls his own sheep by name and leads them out … and the sheep follow him, for they know his voice." In John 14:15–18, Jesus shares with believers what the Holy Spirit is like. He says, "If you love Me, keep My commandments. And I will pray the Father, and He will give you another Helper, that He may abide with you forever—the Spirit of truth, whom the world cannot receive, because it neither sees Him nor knows Him; but you know Him, for He dwells with you and will be in you. I will not leave you as orphans; I will come to you." With these and other words, Jesus prepared his first disciples, and the church today, for the Holy Spirit. Over and over in Scripture, the Holy Spirit is described as a helper, guide, leader, comforter, counselor, and friend (see John 14–16). He encourages His followers to follow Him closely as He leads and gently guides.

As we accept His free gift of salvation by placing our faith in Jesus Christ, through God's grace we can then receive and accept the Holy Spirit's baptism to become Spirit-empowered witnesses for Jesus (see Acts 1:4–8). Through the empowering baptism of the Holy Spirit, a believer can become more sensitive to the leading and guidance of the Master's voice. The Holy Spirit is the one Jesus sent to His church on the day of Pentecost (see Acts 1–2), and He is still baptizing believers with the Holy Spirit today. We can develop our relationship with Him through Bible study and prayer. Whether through His written Word, the gifts of the Holy Spirit, life circumstances, or His still, small voice, believers can develop more sensitivity to the gentle leading of Jesus through the person of the Holy Spirit. And as my puppy Kona learned to be gently led by me, believers can learn to be more and more obedient to the Master's voice and enjoy our walks with Him.

Personal Prayer

Father, I ask you to gently lead and guide me in the direction you want me to go. I pray that the Holy Spirit would baptize me with the power to be an obedient follower of Jesus Christ. Lord, make me sensitive to the gentle guidance of the Holy Spirit, and make your will known to me. Please direct me on your path. Amen.

Focus Verses and Prayers of Faith

Psalm 25:5 Lead me in Your truth and teach me, for you are the God of my salvation; on You I wait all the day. • *God, please lead me in your truth and teach me as I wait on you.*

Psalm 31:3 For You are my rock and my fortress; therefore, for Your name's sake, lead me and guide me. • *I thank you that you are my rock and my fortress, dear God, and that you lead me and guide me.*

Proverbs 3:5–6 Trust in the LORD with all your heart, and lean not on your own understanding; in all your ways acknowledge Him, and He shall direct your paths. • *I trust in the Lord with all my heart, and I do not lean on my own understanding. In all my ways I acknowledge Him, and He will direct my path.*

John 10:2–4, 27 But he who enters by the door is the shepherd of the sheep. To him the doorkeeper opens, and the sheep hear his voice; and he calls his own sheep by name and leads them out. And when he brings out his own sheep, he goes before them; and the sheep follow him, for they know his voice. My sheep hear My voice, and I know them, and they follow Me. • *Thank you, Lord, that I will hear your voice and follow you.*

Devotional Thoughts for Personal Journaling

1. Ask the Lord to bring to mind a time when He clearly guided you. Write down what the process and experience was like. In what ways did He lead

and guide you? Give Him praise and thanks for His guidance.

2. Have you felt distant from the Lord lately, or are you seeking more clear guidance from Him? Journal the following:

    a. What are the best times of day and situations for you to hear from the Lord? What prevents or hinders those times?

    b. How can you be more intentional about drawing near to the Lord in your quiet times? Write down action steps to make those times more frequent in your life.

    c. Ask the Holy Spirit to search your heart. Is there anyone you need to forgive? Sometimes unconfessed sin can keep a believer from being sensitive to God's leading. Take time to ask His help to take steps of forgiveness. Meditate on Matthew 6:13–15 regarding forgiveness.

3. Every believer can receive the baptism of the Holy Spirit to empower their witness for Christ and help them to follow His guidance more closely. Read and study Acts 1–2 and what happened on the day of Pentecost when the believers met together in the upper room. Pray to receive a fresh outpouring of the Holy Spirit in your life.

4

WAIT!

A Lesson in Patience

Wait on the LORD; be of good courage, and He shall strengthen your heart; wait, I say, on the LORD! (Psalm 27:14)

One day I was out walking Joy. I had dropped our daughters off at school and was relishing a walk in a friendly suburban commercial district. The area was pedestrian friendly, complete with nice sidewalks and stoplights, coffee shops, grocery stores, and the like. As I mentioned, I often use my dog-walking time as prayer time. I walk and pray. If people notice, they probably think I'm talking to my dogs! This time, Joy was straining ahead of me, as usual, pulling on her harness. She weighs about fourteen pounds, so I sometimes let her run ahead on her retractable leash. She'd have a hard time pulling me over, so I don't always make her behave as much as I should. As she strained ahead, arriving at the curb first, I gave her the command, "Wait!" The moment I said it, I knew the Holy Spirit was drawing my attention to the word *wait* in my own heart. I could see that there was oncoming traffic that could easily hit and kill Joy instantly if she leapt off the curb before I could pull her back. Joy knew the "wait" command. She had learned how to wait through our patient training of her. We'd give her treats at home if she would wait to eat her dinner until we said she could eat. So, on our walk that day, having been trained to wait, she stopped immediately and looked back at me.

When Joy obeyed me as I commanded her to wait, it was as if the Holy Spirit spoke an impression in my heart: *See, when I make you wait, it's for your safety. I can see ahead of you. I am above and over all of your circumstances. I know the things to come, and so, for your safety and protection, I make you wait.* At five feet eight inches tall, I am far above Joy's height. I can see oncoming traffic. Likewise, God is far above all of our circumstances. He knows all things. He is omniscient (all-knowing), omnipotent (all-powerful), and omnipresent (present everywhere). God knows what dangers and temptations lay ahead of me. His word promises His protection and direction if I trust Him and obey His voice. Proverbs 3:5–7 puts it this way: "Trust in the LORD with all your heart, lean not on your own understanding; in all your ways acknowledge Him, and He shall direct your paths." I shouted, "Wait!" to my little dog Joy on that walk that day because I love her and I was concerned for her safety. Joy had been trained to obey her master's voice, and she was kept safe from those oncoming cars. God, out of his loving concern for our welfare, often says to wait. We want Him to always answer yes to our prayers, but sometimes He says no or simply, *Wait*. He knows all things. He sees ahead of us, into the future. He stands taller than we do and sees above the current circumstances.

If you don't like waiting, you're not alone. Like me, most Americans don't do it very well. America is the land of fast-food restaurants, microwave ovens, and automatic teller machines. The concept of waiting is somewhat foreign, even to those in the church. However, the discipline of waiting upon God and His timing is something that becomes familiar to Christians as their faith deepens and their spiritual walk matures. How? We learn by experiencing the often long, seemingly endless waits for our prayers to be answered. We want everything right away, like a frozen dinner popped into the microwave oven for four minutes. God's answers, however, often come like a serving of stew that's been cooked all day in the Crock-Pot®. A mother making a meal for her family in the slow cooker watches and stirs, and the flavor of the meal slowly develops over time, until at the end of a cold winter's day the stew is ready. Just like that concerned mother, God watches over His children as He slowly develops their trust in Him. Waiting is often difficult when we, in our impatience, want a "quick fix" and answer to our problems uttered in prayer to God.

Learning to wait upon the Lord is not just about answered prayer. It is also about experiencing the presence of the Holy Spirit. We enter into His presence by reading His Word—the Bible—praying, and just waiting. Listening for Him to speak can be lost in our busy, always-in-a-hurry society. But He still speaks. His ways haven't changed. He is ready for us to listen if we will only wait quietly for Him to speak. His Word says in Jeremiah 33:3, "Call to Me, and I will answer you, and show you great and mighty things, which you do not know." To hear God's answer, we need to quiet ourselves before Him, waiting for His still, small voice to speak.

Sometimes God's waiting room is for the development of our character. He refrains from answering our prayers in order to test our character, to help us become more like Him. As we pray and wait, rather than changing those around us who are so "difficult" (in our own estimation), He changes us. I have learned these things through lengthy waiting times in my own life. After saying yes to a call to ministry, in middle age, as a mother of two young daughters, I had to learn to wait upon God and trust Him no matter what. As a full-time mother, I enrolled in Bible training school part-time. My husband, a corporate attorney and sole breadwinner for our family, was suddenly disabled from his job due to a sports injury. What seemed like a routine concussion has become a test of patience for several years as my husband has struggled with postconcussive syndrome (constant headaches, short-term memory loss, and other side effects). I have prayed many prayers for healing and restoration. Often these prayers have seemed unanswered. Looking back over the past several years, however, I can see how God has changed me through the long wait. He has developed and grown my faith, my dependence upon Him, and my trust in Him. He has also stripped away so many carnal desires and replaced them with a resolve to serve Him and to do what is right no matter what the circumstance.

The waiting times in God can also be for our safety. As newer Christians, we can often have more boldness or zeal than wisdom. I know I did. Rushing out ahead of God was one of my greatest weaknesses. The sin of presumption (going ahead of God rather than trusting His timing) can be as dangerous as, or worse than, the sin of disobedience. Disobedience got Jonah into the belly of a whale for three days (see Jonah 1:17), while the sin of presumption landed Joseph in the bottom of a pit and eventually in prison for many years (see the story of Joseph's life found in Genesis 37–50).

To tell Joseph's story briefly, God had given Joseph a prophetic dream of great leadership, but Joseph shared his dream presumptively with his brothers (years before it would come to pass), which led to their jealousy and years of horrible circumstances for Joseph because of their sin against him. Whether these particular scenarios were part of God's original plan for Joseph or not is not clear from the text. Despite Joseph's brash presumption in sharing the prophetic dream, he maintained his integrity during an extended time of suffering. And as Romans 8:28 says, "All things work together for good to those who love God, to those who are the called according to His purpose." God worked everything for Joseph's good in the end. In all of Joseph's difficulty—as he was sold as a slave, falsely accused of a crime, and sent to prison, and through years of waiting—God tested Joseph's character. Joseph passed the test. God, in fact, kept Joseph safe so he could reach his ultimate destiny. After years of waiting, in jail, Joseph was suddenly released and became governor over Egypt to provide food for the very brothers who had betrayed him in their jealousy. Joseph's wait was for his own protection, so God could use him for a great purpose. His prison was his place of protection.

When I was first called to serve the Lord in ministry, I assumed (or rather presumed) like Joseph that I would be running out into the foreign mission field and my destiny of greatness for God right away. But years of small steps of obedience toward ministry preparation and character development have taught me otherwise. After nine years of prayer and holding fast to a dream of missions trips, I finally went on my first two trips to serve on a missions team. I believe that through it all God has protected me, especially from my sometimes overzealous self. Just as Joy, my darling little dog, was protected from traffic that day, so other Christians and I can be protected through obedience to the Master's voice when His answer to our prayers is simply, *Wait!*

Personal Prayer

God, I confess my sin of impatience and ask you to forgive me. Help me to wait patiently for your answers to my prayers. Patience and long-suffering are fruit of your Holy Spirit. Holy Spirit, help me, I pray, and give me the persistence and patience I need to simply wait. Amen.

Focus Verses and Prayers of Faith

Psalm 33:20 Our soul waits for the LORD; He is our help and our shield. • *Thank you that as I wait on you, Lord, you are my help and shield.*

Psalm 37:7 Rest in the LORD, and wait patiently for Him; do not fret because of him who prospers in his way; because of the man who brings wicked schemes to pass. • *As I rest in you, Jesus, I will wait patiently for you.*

Isaiah 40:31 But those who wait on the LORD shall renew their strength; they shall mount up with wings like eagles, they shall run and not be weary, they shall walk and not faint. • *Thank you, Father, that as I wait on you, you renew my strength. I will run and not grow weary. I will walk and not faint.*

James 5:7–8 Therefore be patient, brethren, until the coming of the Lord. See how the farmer waits for the precious fruit of the earth, waiting patiently for it until it receives the early and latter rain. You also be patient. Establish your hearts, for the coming of the Lord is at hand. • *I wait patiently for the Lord, as a farmer waits patiently for the early and the latter rain. I am patient, and my heart is established in Christ.*

Devotional Thoughts for Personal Journaling

1. Have you had a time of seemingly endless waiting for answers to your prayers? How have you sustained your faith during that time? Ask God for His help to wait patiently for His answers. Confess the above prayers of faith as a declaration of your personal faith, and watch Him transform you through His Word.

2. Take time to read through Genesis 37–50. Journal your own observations about Joseph's character and behavior during his time of adversity. How did his moral choices help bring him through a long wait and terrible suffering, into a victorious destiny? Ask God to help you develop those same character traits in yourself.

5

🦴

OBEDIENCE TRAINING
A Lesson in Discipline

My child, don't reject the LORD's discipline, and don't be upset when he corrects you. For the LORD corrects those He loves, just as a father corrects a child in whom he delights. (Proverbs 3:11–12 NLT)

Eventually, Kona and Joy learned to walk together peacefully. Kona no longer sat stubbornly whimpering on the driveway when I would try to take her for a walk. She began to follow along in response to treats and praise. But as she grew, she was getting stronger and stronger. Being a working dog, the Portuguese Water Dog is a natural athlete. Kona could sail through the air off our deck, flying about ten feet as she ran out into the yard. Having previously trained Joy, a natural-born lap dog, I was a little overwhelmed by Kona's high-energy ways. She could leap onto the top of the washing machine (where I foolishly placed the dog treat canister) from a seated position on the floor! She would jump, spring, and leap onto everyone and everything if left to her own devices. There were days I was simply at a loss as to what to do with her.

As I prayed about it, I kept having a recurring thought: obedience training. I had already taken Kona to one puppy kindergarten class (the highest "grade" Joy ever "graduated" from), but the thought persisted. I knew the Holy Spirit was prompting that impression over and over. I kept thinking about all of the reasons I was too busy for doggy obedience classes. Kona clearly needed more obedience training, but there was more to it than that.

I soon realized that the Holy Spirit wasn't just speaking to me about obedience training for my puppy. He began to remind me of all the ways He had trained me in the first ten years of my Christian walk. Obedience training for me, as a Christian and growing disciple, had come through loving pastors and mentors who prayed for and mentored me. As I submitted myself to a godly training and discipleship process, they specifically corrected me when necessary. I had learned, through practice, to be a teachable disciple of Jesus Christ.

Obedience training had also come in my Christian life in the form of my choosing to obey the directions and promptings of the Holy Spirit as well as the precepts found in the Bible. Often those right choices came at great personal expense. Through making right choices, I had developed more of the spiritual "fruit" of self-control referenced by the apostle Paul in Galatians 5:22–23. My spiritual obedience-training program included daily prayer (both "with the spirit and with the understanding" as Paul says in 1 Corinthians 14:15), Bible study, regular church attendance, fellowship with maturing Christian friends, and submission to the authority of godly Christian leaders. I was growing as a disciple of Jesus Christ and into a Christian leader. God showed me that my potential in Christ had been developed over time through these personal spiritual disciplines.

I am not unique. All Christians can grow from newly born-again believers into maturing disciples of Christ. It takes submission to God's spiritual obedience training. Often the biggest cost is our pride. We must humble ourselves before our God, making an honest assessment of our lives and behavior. Repentance often follows serious self-assessment. As I had in my overzealous excitement when I was a new believer, my overzealous puppy needed obedience training!

I enrolled Kona and myself in an obedience class once a week, and we practiced what we learned each day. It was an act of patience and love for me to continually discipline her to listen and obey. Some days I had more patience than others, but training the dog developed the fruit of the Spirit of patience in me. As a Christian, I am learning obedience to the Master's voice. As I trained my dog, the Holy Spirit showed me how He has and is continuing to train me. The dog trainer suggested a prong collar for obedience class. It pinched the puppy's neck when correction was needed, just like their mother would put her mouth on the neck of her pup. The collar provided a gentle but firm correction. I have experienced the very humbling correction of the Holy Spirit. I can relate to my dog's obedience training. It can hurt a little but is very profitable in the end. Hebrews 12:11 says, "Now no chastening seems to be joyful for the present, but painful; nevertheless, afterward it yields the peaceable fruit of righteousness to those who have been trained by it."

As Christians, when we submit ourselves to the Master's training, it is always beneficial to our lives. The same was true as I trained my puppy. She became a better "citizen" in our household. I was even able to walk her to a local coffee shop and have her and Joy lay quietly together under the table while I sipped my tea! Our walks and our daily lives together became more enjoyable as I patiently trained her and she became more obedient. I am also learning to be more obedient to the Master. We all can. We just need a little obedience training.

Personal Prayer

Lord, I repent of those times when I have disobeyed you or disregarded your correction. Please help me to read your Word, pray, and listen to your still, small voice so I may be trained by you and grow in your grace. Amen.

Focus Verses and Prayers of Faith

Revelation 3:19 (MSG) The people I love, I call to account—prod and correct and guide so that they'll live at their best. Up on your feet, then! About face! Run after God! • *Lord, help me to accept your correction and your guidance so I will live at my best.*

Galatians 5:22–23 But the fruit of the Spirit is love, joy, peace, longsuffering, kindness, goodness, faithfulness, gentleness, self-control. • *God, in Jesus' name, I ask you to develop the fruit of the Spirit in my life. I choose to walk in love, joy, peace, longsuffering, kindness, goodness, faithfulness, gentleness, and self-control by your Spirit.*

2 Timothy 3:16 All Scripture is given by inspiration of God, and is profitable for doctrine, for reproof, for correction, for instruction in righteousness. • *The Word of God will reprove, correct, and instruct me in righteousness.*

Hebrews 12:11 Now no chastening seems to be joyful for the present, but painful; nevertheless, afterward it yields the peaceable fruit of righteousness to those who have been trained by it. • *I am trained by the chastening of the Lord, thereby developing the peaceable fruit of righteousness in my life.*

Devotional Thoughts for Personal Journaling

1. Have you had times when the Lord has corrected or disciplined you in some way, either through

His Word, a church leader, or in some other way? Remember that time and journal your reactions to the correction. Looking back on that time, is there anything you could have done differently?

2. Read and memorize 2 Timothy 3:16. Notice in your devotional times over the next several weeks how the Lord uses His Word to train you, correct you, or speak to you. Write down any clear direction or correction you receive from the Lord through His Word.

6

THE GOOD SHEPHERD
A Lesson in God's Care

"I am the good shepherd. The good shepherd gives His life for the sheep. But a hireling, he who is not the shepherd, one who does not own the sheep, sees the wolf coming and leaves the sheep and flees; and the wolf catches the sheep and scatters them. The hireling flees because he is a hireling and does not care about the sheep. I am the good shepherd; and I know My sheep, and am known by My own. As the Father knows Me, even so I know the Father; and I lay down My life for the sheep." (John 10:11–15)

My friend Kaydy has a dog named Sassy. Sassy is a darling black-and-white Border Collie. She has the same name as a little black stray dog my uncle picked up on the side of the road when I was a kid. My childhood dog named Sassy was adopted by our family and outlived two Golden Retrievers. Whenever I go to Kaydy's house, her Sassy is roaming freely around the horse farm where they live. She brings back fond memories of my childhood dog.

This modern-day Sassy is vigilant, always on patrol to keep everyone safe. She has such a shepherding instinct that she even tries to "herd" the horses. Trying to herd a Thoroughbred horse reaching sixteen to seventeen hands high is not a good idea if you are a Border Collie (who stands as tall as the horse's knee at best). Sassy could get herself kicked in the head if she isn't careful. She drinks out of a garden hose and leaps in the air with delight as she is sprayed with water. Sassy can really bring a smile to your face.

My favorite time to watch Sassy is when our kids get into the swimming pool together. Sassy is then on high alert! She patrols the edges of the pool, repeatedly running around the perimeter, watching the kids (and barking at them) to make sure they are safe. She is persistent and stays on lifeguard duty the entire time they are in the water. It could be an hour or more, but she never quits. It is comical to watch Sassy do her "job."

Sassy and her shepherding instinct got me thinking about the biblical illustration of the good shepherd. Jesus called himself the "good shepherd" in John 10:11. There he vividly described the protective efforts of a good shepherd: watching over and protecting his flock of sheep to keep them from harm. He painted a word picture for his audience of Himself protecting and watching over believers as a shepherd watches over and protects his sheep. He pointed out that sheep follow a good shepherd as they are led by his voice. Unlike a hired man, a good shepherd protects his flock and doesn't abandon them when wolves or thieves come. In John 10, John writes of committed believers following Jesus. They are led by His voice and not deceived by the voice of another. Believers are cared for and protected by God, as a good shepherd protects sheep.

The good shepherd analogy is also used by King David, speaking of God, in Psalm 23:1–2: "The Lord is my shepherd; I shall not want." The shepherd (God) is again pictured as a protector and defender of the sheep (believers).

Sassy the dog illustrates a small picture of the good shepherd. She is determined to make sure the kids are safe while they are in the swimming pool. She watches over and protects them. Sassy never quits. Watching Sassy helps me to understand Jesus' illustration of the good shepherd watching over me and all believers. Like Sassy the diligent Border Collie, the Lord watches over you and me. He protects those who belong to Him; He guards them and He never quits.

Personal Prayer

Lord, when I am afraid, help me to remember you are watching over me as a good shepherd watches over his sheep. I thank you that you are caring for, protecting, and providing for me. Amen.

Focus Verses and Prayers of Faith

Psalm 23:1–3 The LORD is my shepherd; I shall not want. He makes me to lie down in green pastures; He leads me beside the still waters. He restores my soul; He leads me in the paths of righteousness for His name's sake. • *Lord, you are my shepherd; thank you that I shall not want for anything. I am following your lead in right paths, and you restore my soul.*

Psalm 91:10–11 No evil shall befall you, nor shall any plague come near your dwelling; for He shall give His angels charge over you, to keep you in all your ways. • *Thank you, Lord, that you send your angels to protect me and keep me safe.*

Psalm 80:1–3 (NLT) Please listen, O Shepherd of Israel, you who lead Joseph's descendants like a flock. O God, enthroned above the cherubim, display your radiant glory to Ephraim, Benjamin, and Manasseh. Show us your mighty power. Come to rescue us! Turn us again to yourself, O God. Make your face shine down upon us. Only then will we be saved. • *Listen to my prayers, Lord! Come to my rescue! Only then will I be saved.*

Devotional Thoughts for Personal Journaling

Looking back on your life, recall a time when you clearly sensed the protection of the Good Shepherd. Write down your memories of that experience. Use it as a memorial to the Lord's goodness in your life. Ask God to give you opportunities to share your life experiences with others to encourage them in their faith. And remember to thank God for His protection.

7

SPRAWLED OUT ON THE COUCH
A Lesson in Rest

Don't worry about anything; instead, pray about everything.
Tell God what you need, and thank him for all he has done.
Then you will experience God's peace, which exceeds anything we can understand. His peace will guard your hearts
and minds as you live in Christ Jesus. (Philippians 4:6–7 NLT)

My dogs know how to rest. One day I walked into our four-season porch to find them both sprawled out comfortably on separate couches. They were both sound asleep, the picture of absolute relaxation. Kona, with her lanky legs, was sprawled on one end, her body contorted in a strange position. Joy, with her more petite frame, was curled in a little ball, nose to tail, on the back of the sofa. She likes to perch on top of the couch to survey the yard for invading squirrels. She must've fallen asleep there in the middle of her guard duty. The photo I took of them became my Facebook status that day with this caption: *My dogs know how to rest*. The other day I went downstairs to let Kona out of her crate, and there she was again. This time on her back, spread-eagle, totally asleep with her limbs flopped in four different directions. I started to laugh out loud. I thought to myself, again, *She knows how to rest!* I wish I could fall asleep that quickly and that easily and that completely—right in the middle of the day! My dogs don't lie tossing and turning, worrying about where the next meal will come from or what's going to happen tomorrow. They just rest. No doubt about it, my dogs know how to rest.

My absolutely relaxed dogs got me to thinking about the "rest of God." Like many believers, I sometimes have trouble remembering that I need to rest in God and trust in Him. Prayer and reading God's Word help me to enter into His place of peace and rest. For example, Jesus invited believers to bring their burdens to Him in Matthew 11:28, which states, "Come to Me, all you who labor and are heavy laden, and I will give you rest." Another admonition to bring our anxieties to God is found in Matthew 6:26–33:

> "Look at the birds of the air, for they neither sow nor reap nor gather into barns; yet your heavenly Father feeds them. Are you not of more value than they? Which of you by worrying can add one cubit to his

stature? So why do you worry about clothing? Consider the lilies of the field, how they grow: they neither toil nor spin; and yet I say to you that even Solomon in all his glory was not arrayed like one of these. Now if God so clothes the grass of the field, which today is, and tomorrow is thrown into the oven, will He not much more clothe you, O you of little faith? Therefore do not worry, saying, 'What shall we eat?' or 'What shall we drink?' or 'What shall we wear?' For after all these things the Gentiles seek. For your heavenly Father knows that you need all these things. But seek first the kingdom of God and His righteousness, and all these things shall be added to you."

In such a poignant and powerful way, Jesus painted a word picture for His audience of His Father's ability to provide for His children who trust Him. So, Jesus encouraged us to seek God's will and God's direction first. When we do so, we can trust Him to provide for our needs. That knowledge and assurance brings us peace beyond our understanding. The peace of God helps us to enter into His rest. I believe that is what the psalmist was referring to when he said in Psalm 91:1, "He who dwells in the secret place of the Most High shall abide under the shadow of the Almighty." When we are seeking God's will first in our lives, and we prayerfully follow His leading, He will show us what to do. We can simply rest in the knowledge of His provision, care, and protection.

I am a good master for my dogs. I do my best to make sure they are fed and cared for, walked regularly, and played with. In short, I take care of their needs, with the help of my family. My dogs just relax, knowing their needs will be met. I believe God used my resting dogs to remind me I can trust Him to take care of me. If I truly believe His Word, I can enter into His rest every day, no matter what season of life I am in or what challenges I may face. I can enter into the rest of God anytime, anyplace, with His Holy Spirit's help. If I forget to pray and spend time in His Word, I can become fretful and anxious. Even my prayers can become demanding and anxiety ridden. But, if I spend time in worship, in His Word, and in prayer every day, I can go through the busiest of days in the sure knowledge of His care and provision.

Of course, some days and seasons of life are busier than others. We cannot always literally flop on the couch like our dogs. Some of the greatest times of God's peace in my life have come during seasons of terrible grief or persecution by unbelievers. As I sought the Lord intensely during the worst times, His peace surrounded me. We can always enter God's rest with the help of the Holy Spirit through prayer.

When I think of my two dogs flopped sleepily on my couch, the picture of perfect relaxation, it reminds me to enter into God's rest. I remind myself I can call upon His Holy Spirit to help my spirit to simply rest in Him and trust in Him no matter what comes. You can too.

Personal Prayer

Father, I confess to you that I sometimes dwell in a place of anxiety for far too long. I am sorry for those times when I haven't taken the time to seek you and your solutions to my problems. I pray, in Jesus' name, that you would help me to trust in you and rest in you. Amen.

Focus Verses and Prayers of Faith

Psalm 91:1 Those who live in the shelter of the Most High will find rest in the shadow of the Almighty. · *Thank you, Lord, that I dwell in the secret place of the Most High and I rest under the shadow of the Almighty.*

Psalm 37:6–8 He shall bring forth your righteousness as the light, and your justice as the noonday. Rest in the LORD, and wait patiently for Him; do not fret because of him who prospers in his way, because of the man who brings wicked schemes to pass. Cease from anger, and forsake wrath; do not fret—it only causes harm. · *I choose to rest in the Lord and wait patiently for Him. I will not fret, because I choose the peace of Christ.*

Matthew 11:28 "Come to Me, all you who labor and are heavy laden, and I will give you rest." · *God, help me to bring all of my heavy burdens to you and exchange them for your rest.*

Devotional Thoughts for Personal Journaling

1. In your own life, where have you seen progress in moving from a place of anxiety to a place of more peace? Write down these areas of victory, and thank God for the progress!

2. What specific situations cause you to become anxious and restless? How can you consciously help yourself to remain "restful" in God during these times? Journal an action plan and pray over it. Consider asking a trusted friend to hold you accountable to your action plan, particularly in an area of habitual struggle.

8

SEATED ON THE MASTER'S LAP

A Lesson in the Position of the Believer

And God raised us up with Christ and seated us with him in the heavenly realms in Christ Jesus. (Ephesians 2:6 NIV)

I know someone who knows exactly to whom she belongs. My little dog Joy. As a Cavachon, her entire genetic family history (both the Bichon Frisé and Cavalier King Charles Spaniel) is dedicated primarily to one purpose: sitting on a master's lap. Cavaliers were the famed lap dogs of English kings. Go to any sidewalk café in France and you're sure to see a pampered Bichon Frisé seated with its owner.

Joy knows her purpose in life, and she lives it to the fullest. She sits on our laps as often as she is allowed. There is no place she would rather be. One of my favorite times of day is when I get up in the early morning to pray and read the Bible.

I sneak downstairs to make a cup of tea, and there she is waiting next to my prayer chair. As I sit down to read, Joy makes it clear she wants to be in her rightful position. I routinely have to move my Bible out of her way so she can jump onto my lap. If I don't, she'll just jump right on top of it. If I try to get her to sit next to me, she nudges my hand with her nose until I make room for her on my lap. Once she is comfortably seated in her master's lap, I can then set my Bible on top of her in order to read it. She snuggles in while I read and pray. Joy knows that she belongs to me, and from her perch on my lap, she surveys the room to see what is happening or just falls asleep. Joy knows that seated with me, her master, she is safe.

How about you? Do you know your purpose? Do you know to whom you belong and by whom you have been adopted? The apostle Paul declares the position of all believers in Christ in the opening chapters of his letter to the church at Ephesus. Ephesians 2:6 states, "And God raised us up with Christ and seated us with him in the heavenly realms in Christ Jesus" (NIV). In Ephesians 1:5, Paul also speaks of believers, stating that there is spiritual "adoption" that occurs when we believe and trust Christ as our Savior. Paul's eloquent greeting and declaration of the positional authority of the believer is worth reading and re-reading. In Ephesians 1:6, Paul emphatically states that the believer is "accepted in the Beloved." The biblically based knowledge of our full acceptance by God, when we trust Christ, is key to understanding our security as believers. If, as believers, we can grasp the fact that we are adopted into the family of the King of Kings, we won't walk in insecurity about eternity, in fear, shame, guilt, or self-condemnation any longer. With the Holy Spirit's help, we can begin to understand the freedom Paul had. He knew who he was in Christ, and he knew his purpose was to glorify Christ. It is that unshakable confidence that brought Paul through stonings by a mob, trials before Caesar, a tempest at sea, and imprisonment for his faith (see Acts 9–28).

As a newer Christian, I struggled with many forms of insecurity. Fear-based rather than faith-based behaviors were the norm. My fears were many. Fear of failure, fear of what others thought of my newfound faith, and shame-based fears related to past sin. While God clearly forgives and forgets all sin once confessed and repented of, people are not always so quick to forgive. Hence, I tended to live in shame over things God had already forgotten! All that fear and shame kept me from fully walking in Christ's peace. Gradually, however, I began to understand who I was in Christ. Through Bible reading, praying in the Spirit (the gift of other tongues as found in Acts 2), spending time with more mature believers, praying Bible verses, and attending group Bible study, those fears began to melt away. I founded a women's ministry at my church based on Ephesians 1:6, "accepted in the Beloved," because the Holy Spirit showed me that He wanted many more women to have the same victory that I was beginning to have over the feelings of insecurity, fear, and rejection. I called that first ministry, "Beloved Women's Ministry." What God was teaching me, I began to teach others. I am still learning and growing more confident in my identity in Christ day by day.

The apostle Paul knew he was beloved by Christ, and he wrote to the Ephesian church and to us so that we would know that too. On that sure foundation of Christ's love, his faith became unshakable. How about you? Do you know that you belong to Christ? Do you understand the depths of God's love for you? Let the Holy Spirit soak that knowledge into your heart by reading, memorizing, and praying God's Word. The Holy Spirit used my little lap dog Joy to remind me that all those who belong to Christ are seated in the Master's lap. We are beloved by Him. In that sure knowledge, we are safe and secure.

Personal Prayer

Lord, forgive me for sometimes forgetting that I belong to you. Help me to bring my insecurities and fears to you and exchange them for your peace. God, help me to more fully understand your love for me. Please remind me I am seated on the Master's lap. Amen.

Focus Verses and Prayers of Faith

Romans 8:15 For you did not receive the spirit of bondage again to fear, but you received the Spirit of adoption by whom we cry out, "Abba, Father." · *Thank you, Lord, that I am not in* *bondage to fear, but I have received the Spirit of adoption by which I cry out, "Abba, Father."*

Ephesians 2:4–6 But God, who is rich in mercy, because of His great love with which He loved us, even when we were dead in trespasses, made us alive together with Christ (by grace you have been saved), and raised us up together, and made us sit together in the heavenly places in Christ Jesus. · *Lord, I praise you that I am seated with Christ in heavenly places far above all principalities and powers.*

Ephesians 1:6 He made us accepted in the Beloved. · *God, I am so grateful that I am accepted in the Beloved. Help me to be ever more secure in that knowledge.*

Devotional Thoughts for Personal Journaling

1. Do you struggle with any fears or insecurities? Pray for the Holy Spirit to reveal any areas of your own insecurity. Focus on declaring the above prayers of faith and find other verses that speak to your situation. Journal the progress you see in this area of your life as you pray regularly about it.

2. With God's help, focus on praying for a renewed sense of your own purpose and destiny. Pray and ask God how He can use you to bring glory to Christ in your home, school, workplace, or church. If you've had a God-given dream that died, ask God to give you renewed vision and

purpose. Set your sights on your position in Christ and decide to view life's challenges from His perspective, far above all principalities and powers. Journal the revelations you receive and a personal plan to take steps toward their fulfillment.

9

AN INVISIBLE FENCE
A Lesson in God's Protection through His Word

Your word is a lamp to my feet and a light to my path.
(Psalm 119:105)

In our yard we have an underground electric dog fence set to the same frequency as the electric collar our dogs wear. The brand name is Invisible Fence®. Our dogs had to be trained to stay in our yard using treat incentives and white flags placed along the fence line, along with the help of a professional trainer. Every time they would get near the flags, the collar would beep, giving them an audible warning before they actually got a mild shock. I would take the treats and say, "Stay in the yard," as the trainer had instructed me. I would then run into the center of the yard, and when they followed, I would give them plenty of praise along with a training treat. When they got it right, they never got a shock, but when they wandered too close to the edge of the fence zone, they would yelp! They would get a mild jolt of electric shock, and they quickly learned that staying away from the boundary line was a much more positive experience. This may seem cruel to some, until you consider the alternatives.

The electric dog fence gave our dogs total freedom to run around and play in our yard without being tied up. They just rang their bells on the door that I have trained them to ring in order to let us know they need to go outside to go potty. Then they were free to go to the bathroom and romp around the yard to their heart's content. The electric fence and collar system kept our dogs from straying into the street and being hit by a car, running away, or getting attacked by coyotes, which occasionally pass through the woodsy edges of our suburban neighborhood. The invisible electric fence provided a safe boundary for our dogs, and they had total freedom within the safety of its borders.

When I was a child, we had a hobby farm with horses, dogs, cats, an occasional turtle, canary, goldfish, or other miscellaneous pets. The horses were kept in their pasture by an aboveground, visible electric fence. It didn't take long for them, or us kids, to realize that a jolt from the fence was unpleasant. Having gotten a few zaps while crawling under the horse fence, I can say it was uncomfortable enough to make one unwilling to repeat the experience. There was a definite disincentive for the horses to get too near that fence or to attempt to escape their safe pasture. Similarly, our dogs have learned to stay in our yard.

During that time in my life, my cousins also owned horses. We would ride together every summer. Unfortunately, one of their horses jumped the fence one night. She was a beautiful bay mare named Tira. I still remember the phone call we got telling us that a car had hit Tira in the middle of the night. The fence was meant for her protection, but when she left the safety of her pasture, she was killed instantly on the highway just outside the fence line.

Similar to the horse fence and the invisible electric dog fence, God's Word provides protective boundaries for people. His Word is full of wisdom for everyday living, ranging from advice about having healthy relationships to effectively managing our finances. By reading the Bible often, with the Holy Spirit's illumination, we can learn through both the right and wrong choices of Bible figures how we should live. God's Word clearly teaches that obedience brings blessings. For example, in the book of Genesis we see that Noah chose to obey the Lord's voice and build an ark. The result was that Noah's family was spared from death in the great flood. Also in Genesis, Joseph, though the victim of unjust accusation and terrible mistreatment by his own brothers, chose to obey God's directive regarding forgiveness. He forgave his undeserving brothers out of obedience to God, thereby saving their lives and bringing about family reconciliation. In both cases, choosing to obey God brought lifesaving blessings.

In addition to these types of examples, there are directive words that, when obeyed, bring blessing. For example, Romans 13:12–14 (NLT) says:

> The night is almost gone; the day of salvation will soon be here. So remove your dark deeds like dirty clothes, and put on the shining armor of right living. Because we belong to the day, we must live decent lives for all to see. Don't participate in the darkness of wild parties and drunkenness, or in sexual promiscuity and immoral living, or in quarreling and jealousy. Instead, clothe yourself with the presence of the Lord Jesus Christ. And don't let yourself think about ways to indulge your evil desires.

Every person has a choice to make to obey or disobey God's Word. These specific verses are just a few, among many, that advise against drinking alcohol to the point of drunkenness or participating in sexual immorality, among other sins. The consequences of ignoring these wise admonitions can be severe. For example, if one is sexually promiscuous, one can be infected with a sexually transmitted disease. Similarly, if one chooses to become intoxicated with alcohol and then drive a car, tragedy could result. Neither of those terrible consequences are God's will, because His Word specifically recommends against those behaviors. People who blame God for the consequences of their own sin or the sinful choices of others have not read or understood God's wisdom available through His Word. He does not force people to obey His Word. The Bible says that to every man, God gave a conscience, which helps even those who don't have access to a Bible know right from wrong. The choice between obedience and disobedience is ours.

God's Word provides an invisible fence of protection for humankind. He gives us standards for living because of His great love. His Word gives us healthy boundaries for living, within which we will be safer and more joyful than if we choose to disobey Him. Staying within the safe boundaries of His love by choosing to follow His precepts will always lead to more peace and more joy in this life.

God's Word helps believers to make wise choices that keep them safe in His care. Like a good dog owner who provides their pet a safe place to play, God will send His Holy Spirit as a "trainer" of sorts to help Christians obey His Word and stay within the invisible fence of His protection.

Personal Prayer

God, I ask you to forgive me for times when I have strayed outside your protective boundaries. Thank you for your forgiveness and mercy. Help me to read, understand, and be guided by your Word. I need the Holy Spirit's help to obey you, Lord. Thank you for providing your protection for me. Amen.

Focus Verses and Prayers of Faith

Psalm 91:4 He shall cover you with His feathers, and under His wings you shall take refuge; His truth shall be your shield and buckler. · *You cover me with your feathers, Lord; under your wings I shall take refuge; the truth of your Word shall be my shield.*

Ephesians 6:13–17 Therefore take up the whole armor of God, that you may be able to withstand in the evil day, and having done all, to stand. Stand therefore, having girded your waist with truth, having put on the breastplate of righteousness, and having shod your feet with the preparation of the gospel of peace; above all, taking the shield of faith with which you will be able to quench all the fiery darts of the wicked one. And take the helmet of salvation, and the sword of the Spirit, which is the word of God. · *I choose to put on the armor of God, according to your Word, so I can stand against evil. I put on my waist the belt of truth; I take up the breastplate of the righteousness of Jesus Christ. I put upon my feet the gospel of peace, and I walk in peace. I take up the helmet of my salvation in Christ and the sword of the Holy Spirit, which is the Word of God.*

Hebrews 4:12 For the word of God is living and powerful, and sharper than any two-edged sword, piercing even to the division of soul and spirit, and of joints and marrow, and is a discerner of the thoughts and intents of the heart. · *Your*

Word is living and powerful and sharper than any sword. I believe and pray that your Word would discern and change the thoughts and intents of my heart.

Devotional Thoughts for Personal Journaling

1. Have you ever experienced a time of "straying" outside of God's protection? Compare and contrast that to a time of obedience in your life. How did those times differ, and what did you learn from them?

2. Share, through journaling, which areas of your life you need to come back into the invisible fence of God's protection. Pray through and write down specific steps to success in these areas of your life. Ask a close Christian friend to keep you accountable in these areas to help you have success.

10

🦴

WHILE I WAS SLEEPING, GOD WAS WORKING

A Lesson in the Power of Prayer

The angel of the Lord encamps all around those who fear Him, and delivers them. (Psalm 34:7)

While I was sleeping, God was at work. It was unusual for me to sleep until eight on a Thursday morning. Usually I'd be up at six getting ready to take my kids to school. But that day, our girls didn't have school. I didn't find out what happened until later.

I should preface my story with this. I pray about everything. Philippians 4:6 says, "Don't worry about anything; instead, pray about everything. Tell God what you need, and thank him for all he has done" (NLT). I try to put that into practice in my life. One of the things I pray for, in addition to my own family, is our dog Joy. I regularly pray for her and pet

67

her and ask God to bless and protect her. I pray specifically that she'll live a long, healthy life. She really lives up to her name. She brings joy everywhere that she goes.

That morning as our girls and I slept late, my husband was reading the newspaper on the front porch. He told me later that he hadn't noticed Joy wasn't wearing her electric collar. As it turned out, our invisible fence had been broken, but we were unaware of it.

Our kids go to a Christian school, but the local public schools were in session that day. As a school bus drove down our street, Joy ran to the edge of our yard to bark at it as usual. This time, however, she ran through her invisible fence, out of the yard, and into the path of the oncoming school bus. On her own at only fourteen pounds, she didn't stand a chance.

As my husband watched in horror, the school bus ran over Joy. He was expecting the worst. But, God! The bus ran straight over Joy without one wheel touching her! She shot straight back into the yard, up onto the front porch, and to the front door. She was shaking but otherwise totally unharmed. Not one hair on her furry little head was touched. That was nothing short of a miracle!

When my husband told me the story later that morning, he was astonished. Immediately, a Bible verse I had memorized sprang into my mind. Psalm 34:7 states, "The angel of the LORD encamps all around those who fear Him, and delivers them." As I heard the story about the near miss for my beloved dog, a peace swept over me as that Bible verse came to mind at that precise moment. I knew in my heart that God had answered my prayers and sent an angel to protect our little dog. When our younger daughter heard the story later, she said the very same thing to her Dad, "God sent an angel to protect Joy!"

This has served as such a stark reminder that God hears and answers prayers of all kinds. We can pray about everything in our lives, the small and the big. God has chosen to work through prayer, and we are reminded to "pray about everything" in Philippians 4:6. When we truly pray about everything, we can rest and trust that God has heard and will answer. There is a famous old hymn of the church with the lyric, "His eye is on the sparrow, and I know He watches me."* In this case, His eye was on our dog Joy while I was sleeping.

Personal Prayer

Lord, help me to remember that you care about every detail of my life and that I can truly pray about everything. There is nothing that is too small for your attention. I pray that I would know your loving kindness even more deeply today, and remember to bring my concerns to you.

---

* "His Eye Is on the Sparrow," a hymn written by Civilla D. Martin and Charles H. Gabriel, 1905.

Focus Verses and Prayers of Faith

Philippians 4:6–7 (NLT) Don't worry about anything; instead, pray about everything. Tell God what you need, and thank him for all he has done. Then you will experience God's peace, which exceeds anything we can understand. His peace will guard your hearts and minds as you live in Christ Jesus. · *Lord, I thank you that I am not anxious about anything; instead, I pray about everything. I thank you now for the answers to my prayers, according to your will.*

James 5:13–16 Is anyone among you suffering? Let him pray. Is anyone cheerful? Let him sing psalms. Is anyone among you sick? Let him call for the elders of the church, and let them pray over him, anointing him with oil in the name of the Lord. And the prayer of faith will save the sick, and the Lord will raise him up. And if he has committed sins, he will be forgiven. Confess your trespasses to one another, and pray for one another, that you may be healed. The effective, fervent prayer of a righteous man avails much. · *I thank you, Father, that my prayers are effective and fervent because I have been made righteous by the blood of Jesus.*

Devotional Thoughts for Personal Journaling

1. Do you need a reinvigorated prayer life? Read and declare the above verses on prayer, committing Philippians 4:6–7 to memory. Write it on a note card and glance at it throughout the day to help

you memorize it. Ask the Holy Spirit to help you put it into practice, praying frequently throughout the day. Record your specific prayer requests along with specific answers you receive.

2. Commit (or recommit) yourself to a daily quiet time of Bible reading and listening prayer before God. Begin with fifteen minutes at the beginning or end of your day. Increase that time as you are able. Ask God to help you to keep your daily appointment with Him. After you read the Bible and pray, listen quietly for any impressions from the Holy Spirit. Keep a journal of your impressions. Test them against Scripture.

11

THE LOST DOG

A Lesson in the Compassion of Christ

"What man of you, having a hundred sheep, if he loses one of them, does not leave the ninety-nine in the wilderness, and go after the one which is lost until he finds it? And when he has found it, he lays it on his shoulders, rejoicing. And when he comes home, he calls together his friends and neighbors, saying to them, 'Rejoice with me, for I have found my sheep which was lost!' I say to you that likewise there will be more joy in heaven over one sinner who repents than over ninety-nine just persons who need no repentance." (Luke 15:4–7)

As I drove into our neighborhood one cold, early spring night, I saw a small animal dart past the periphery of my headlights. I did a double take as I thought, *Was that a dog?* I pulled the car over to the side of our street and got out. There in the shadows of a neighbor's house was a tiny dog. I'd never seen him before, and there were no lights on at any of my neighbor's homes. I just knew he must be lost. I called him several times, and he just darted out of sight into the night. *Poor little fella. I hope he doesn't freeze.* I left our garage door open a few inches and the light on all night, just in case he was brave enough to seek refuge in our garage. At least he would be a bit warmer.

The next morning, I saw no sign of him. But, a few days later, as I looked out our front door, there he was again, trotting down our street. In the daylight, I noticed the little dog was skin and bone. Wearing a tattered collar but no tag, he was ragged and unwashed. Clearly he was a lost pet.

For the next three days, my daughters and I tried to catch him. If I called to him, he immediately ran away. We put dog food out on the sidewalk, leaving a trail up to our front porch, hoping we would be able to capture him. It was still very cold, and I worried he would die of exposure or starvation. As he got used to eating the food we left out, my daughters sat on the sidewalk with food in their hands. At one point, he came close enough to eat from their hands. But the poor little dog was so skittish he would bolt if they made any move to try to pet him or grab his collar. We put a dog crate on the front porch with food inside and a water dish nearby. He came and ate from it several times, but none of us could get near enough to get ahold of him. He was so fearful he would instantly run away whenever we tried to go near him. Eventually I borrowed a live trap from a friend in an effort to catch him so we could get him to a place of safety. I even cooked bacon, left the front door open, and set it inside the trap, but to no avail.

Finally, one by one, members of our family went walking or driving through our neighborhood, calling for the little lost dog. I felt an ache in my heart for him. I imagined that a little boy or girl was somewhere praying for him to come home. I wanted to help return him to his owners or to adopt him ourselves. I couldn't stand the thought that he might die out there alone in the cold.

One day, as I walked our own dog in the biting cold, snow-flakes began to fall. I was scanning the neighborhood for any sign of the lost dog, when the Holy Spirit spoke in the quiet of my heart. He simply said, *That's how I feel about the lost people who are far from me. I long to have them return to me. I do not despise them or hate them, instead I long for them to come home.* Immediately Luke's words from chapter 15 flooded my mind. He wrote in verses 4–5, "If a man has a hundred sheep and one of them gets lost, what will he do? Won't he leave the ninety-nine others in the wilderness and go to search for the one that is lost until he finds it? And when he has found it, he will joyfully carry it home on his shoulders" (NLT). I nearly wept there in the cold, looking for the little stray house pet, knowing the Lord's longing for people who were far from Him to come to faith in Jesus Christ. I prayed, repenting of wrong attitudes and asking for His heart for the lost souls all around me. God had used that little lost dog to remind me of His great compassion. As it turned out, several neighbors had been searching for the lost dog, too, but no one ever knew what became of that little dog.

How about you? Do you need to see others as God sees them? Do you need His compassion for the lost people all around you? Like a fearful, skinny stray dog running from the hands that could help shelter, feed, and care for him, so are the many people who are running from God's love and forgiveness. He wants to embrace them with His love, but in fear, sin, and shame, they keep running from God. They simply do not realize the forgiveness, freedom, grace, and mercy that God offers them through Jesus Christ. Perhaps you could be one who goes after the lost with Christ's compassion and shares the good news of Jesus Christ trying to bring them back to a place of safety.

Personal Prayer

Lord, I confess to you that I am often unconcerned and lack compassion for those around me who do not know Jesus Christ by faith. Can you help me to have your compassion and mercy toward them? Lord, give me courage to pursue them with your love and to persist in that mission.

Focus Verses and Prayers of Faith

Luke 15:8–10 "Or what woman, having ten silver coins, if she loses one coin, does not light a lamp, sweep the house, and search carefully until she finds it? And when she has found it, she calls her friends and neighbors together, saying, 'Rejoice with me, for I have found the piece which I lost!' Likewise, I say to you, there is joy in the presence of the angels of God over one sinner who repents." • *Lord, help me to become more diligent to look for the lost around me like the woman who searches diligently for her lost coin. Help me to have your joy in my heart when even one sinner repents. I thank you now for your diligence to seek the lost and your joy when they are found.*

Luke 15:20–24 "And he arose and came to his father. But when he was still a great way off, his father saw him and had compassion, and ran and fell on his neck and kissed him. And the son said to him, 'Father, I have sinned against heaven and in your sight, and am no longer worthy to be called your son.'

"But the father said to his servants, 'Bring out the best robe and put it on him, and put a ring on his hand and sandals on his feet. And bring the fatted calf here and kill it, and let us eat and be merry; for this my son was dead and is alive again; he was lost and is found.' And they began to be merry." • *Father, I thank you for your compassion to open my arms and love the sinners who are turning from their sin and coming into your kingdom. Help me to welcome them with open arms.*

Devotional Thoughts for Personal Journaling

Have you prayed for people, perhaps for a long time, but they are still running from God? Have you given up hope? Ask the Lord to show you where your heart has become hardened and callous toward the sinners in your world. Pray for Him to give you a fresh touch of compassion from the Holy Spirit to continue to pray for and share Christ with them with perseverance and faith. Make a list of those you are seeking renewed compassion to pray for and share Christ with, as the Spirit leads.

12

🦴

CANDY'S HEART
A Lesson in Faith

Faith is the substance of things hoped for, the evidence of things not seen. (Hebrews 11:1)

Candy is a spunky little West Highland White Terrier who belongs to one of my nieces. They have been constant companions for many years as they go about doing chores on the horse farm where they live. Compared to the large, athletic horses that live on the farm, Candy is pretty small. In fact, she's not quite halfway up to the knee of one of those huge horses, if you put them side by side. But what Candy lacks in stature, she makes up for in her disposition. She's all heart. When I visit the farm, she bounces down the front steps, tail wagging in a friendly greeting. She's always cheerful, and it just brightens your day to visit Candy.

It came as quite a shock one night when my niece sent

me an urgent text message asking for prayer for her beloved pet. Candy had developed a serious heart condition called chordae tendinae rupture and congestive heart failure, and her survival hung in the balance. My niece happens to be a veterinary medicine student, so I'm sure she understood the gravity of Candy's condition more than most. In fact, most people probably would have accepted that Candy wouldn't make it. Nevertheless, in her prayer request, I discerned a real gift of faith. Her faith demonstrated Hebrews 11:1 perfectly. "Now faith is the substance of things hoped for, the evidence of things not seen." Contrary to the evidence and well aware of the dire straits that Candy was in, she reached out for God's hand to guide the veterinary care being given to her darling dog. That's what faith is. Faith reaches out to other believers for prayer in spite of the evidence.

Needless to say, I went to prayer, asking the Lord to bless the faith of my niece and put His healing hand upon Candy's heart. I texted several other dog-loving, faith-filled friends, as well, asking them to pray for Candy. Over the next few days, I prayed several times, and I know my friends did too. I got text messages saying, *How's Candy? I'm praying*, and the like. It was nip and tuck for a while, but Candy made it. At nearly fourteen years old, she has survived for more than two additional years with the intervention of God and excellent veterinary care, because of the faith of a girl who reached out for prayer and asked God to do the impossible.

Personal Prayer

Lord, I need your help to see through eyes of faith. I ask you to open my eyes to the possibilities with you rather than seeing the impossible. Thank you, Lord, for giving me eyes to see.

Focus Verses and Prayers of Faith

Hebrews 11:1 Now faith is the substance of things hoped for, the evidence of things not seen. • *Lord, help me to see the invisible, by faith, and pray.*

Hebrews 11:6 But without faith it is impossible to please Him, for he who comes to God must believe that He is, and that He is a rewarder of those who diligently seek Him. • *I believe you are the one who can answer any prayer according to your will, no matter the odds, Lord.*

James 1:6 But let him ask in faith, with no doubting, for he who doubts is like a wave of the sea driven and tossed by the wind. • *I declare and believe that my prayers will be prayers of faith, not of doubt. Help me to trust, believe, and pray in faith, Lord.*

Devotional Thoughts for Personal Journaling

1. Recall a time when you've been faced with the reality of great difficulty or impossibility, whether in a small or large life circumstance. Did you ask

others to pray with you about that circumstance?
What happened? Write down your journey of
faith as a way of remembering God's goodness.

2. Build your faith by memorizing the above Bible
    verses. Write them down on a note card and take
    them with you as you go about your day, until you
    have them memorized.

13

🦴

JUST SAY NO
A Lesson in Spiritual Warfare

Therefore submit to God. Resist the devil and he will flee from you. (James 4:7)

My little Cavachon, Joy, and I were out for a walk on a beautiful summer's evening. She trotted along next to me, her usual happy self. As we rounded a bend in the sidewalk and headed up a hill, I suddenly noticed a large black dog with its tail erect staring at us. I didn't like the looks of his stance. He began to run toward us, with his owner casually walking behind, stating how friendly he was. I had an inner sense he was anything but friendly, in spite of his owner's words.

The dog charged out of his yard, came onto the sidewalk, and towered over my little pet. He gave a few casual sniffs then turned to walk away. Suddenly, however, he turned back toward Joy with teeth bared, ready to snap! There was no time to run, and in a split second I knew that would make matters worse. I looked that dog in the eye, stepped boldly toward him, and shouted, "No!" right in his face. He startled and stopped his attack. By that time his owner had reached us and began pulling her so-called friendly pet back into her yard, apologizing profusely.

As we began to walk on, both Joy and I were a bit shaken. I reassured her with loving pats and kind words. I continued to pray and recognized that the incident with the big black dog was a lot like spiritual warfare (the unseen battle between God's holy angels and satan's demons played out through earthly circumstances or people). The devil comes to tempt or attack Christians or their loved ones, often when they least expect it, and disguised in seemingly innocuous ways. However, the Holy Spirit can help believers to have an inner sense that something is amiss, as I did out on my dog walk that night. Because I was listening to the Holy Spirit's prompting in my heart instead of the dog owner's voice, I was able to quickly step into the path of that aggressive dog, shouting "No!" and preventing a sure bite. Jesus did the same thing to satan in the face of his wilderness temptations as detailed in Luke 4. When the devil tempted Jesus, the Lord spoke directly back to him using the Word of God as a spiritual weapon. He overcame the devil with His Word! Jesus wasn't passive; He actively resisted the devil, and we need to do the same. Through daily prayer, Bible reading, memorizing Scripture, and practicing the Lord's presence, the Christian can begin to see unseen or disguised dangers intended to harm their friends or family and just say no in prayer!

Personal Prayer

Lord, I believe your Word is truth and that I can use it as a spiritual weapon as you did. Help me to use your Word as a weapon.

Focus Verses and Prayers of Faith

James 4:7 Therefore submit to God. Resist the devil and he will flee from you. · *I will resist the devil, and he will flee from me.*

Ephesians 6:10–13 Finally, my brethren, be strong in the Lord and in the power of His might. Put on the whole armor of God, that you may be able to stand against the wiles of the devil. For we do not wrestle against flesh and blood, but against principalities, against powers, against the rulers of the darkness of this age, against spiritual hosts of wickedness in the heavenly places. Therefore take up the whole armor of God, that you may be able to withstand in the evil day, and having done all, to stand. · *I choose to take up the whole armor of God, that I may be able to withstand in the evil day, and having done all, to stand.*

Devotional Thoughts for Personal Journaling

1. Have you ever experienced an inner sense that something was wrong? Did you listen to that

prompting and pray and take action, or fail to take action? Write down what that time was like, what you did right, and what you could have done better. Use it as a reminder to listen to the inner promptings of the Holy Spirit and just say no to the devil!

2. Read 1 Corinthians 12:4–11. Notice verse 10 is the gift of discerning of spirits. Ask the Lord to give you this gift and also a prayer partner with this gift, so you can more effectively watch and pray to bring about the Lord's will rather than the enemy's plan in your life.

14

WOOF, WOOF, WOOF!
A Lesson in Not Giving Up

Yet because of his persistence he will rise and give him as many as he needs. (Luke 11:8)

Having assembled my usual cup of tea, Bible, paper, and pen, I finally sat down to write. I had just gotten comfortable to pray, read the Scriptures, and begin another chapter, when I heard a sound outside the front door. A small *woof* drifted to my ears from our front porch. Having just begun a new story, I ignored Joy's soft bark and kept writing. It wasn't long before I heard it again. "Woof," she barked, this time a little louder. I was in the middle of a stream of writing, and it was a beautiful day outside, so I continued to write. I tend to get in the flow of my writing and tune out the world around me. I was on a roll, writing a new devotion, and I wanted to stay in the stream of thought.

In a couple of minutes, I heard a louder, more insistent *woof* from outside the front door. Joy was persisting in her request to come back inside our house. I knew she wasn't going to give up and take a nap on the front porch, as I'd hoped, so I got up and let her in. She happily trotted into the house, stationing herself on the back of the couch for her afternoon nap. I went back to writing and all was well. I completed the project despite the interruption. It wasn't long, though, before my mind turned back to Joy's increasingly insistent *woofs* outside the front door. As I read my Bible and prayed, I thought about her *woof, woof, woof* as a model for prayer. Let me explain.

I was reading Luke 11, where Jesus taught His disciples about prayer. First, He gave them a pattern to use in the Lord's Prayer, and then He taught them about the importance of persistence through the parable of the persistent friend, found in Luke 11:5–8. There Jesus likened His heavenly Father to a man who's just gotten himself and his family tucked into bed for the night after a long, tiring day. Any parent with young children knows that this can be quite an accomplishment, particularly in close quarters. Suddenly, at midnight the homeowner's sleep is disturbed by a knock on the door by a friend in need. Reluctant to disturb his family and get out of bed, thereby waking his whole household, he refuses the request. However, the friend persists in his request, ultimately succeeding in his pursuit of assistance from the homeowner. Jesus uses the story to teach us that prayer is not a passive or singular exercise. He encourages believers, through this and other parables, to persist on the stubborn points in prayer. Don't get me wrong. God is not unwilling to answer His children's pleas. However, the nature of this present age and the reality of spiritual warfare in the fallen world we live in necessitate faith-filled, persistent prayer. Jesus knew that, of course, which is why He gave us this parable. Like the persistent friend in Jesus' parable and my insistent dog outside my front door that day, believers who persist in their faith-filled prayers are sure to get an answer in line with God's will.

Personal Prayer

Lord, I confess that I can be distracted and easily discouraged over circumstances in my life and easily give up. Help me to be persistent and keep faith that you are working and will answer my prayers according to your will.

Focus Verses and Prayers of Faith

Luke 11:8 (AMP) "I tell you, even though he will not get up and give him anything just because he is his friend, yet because of his persistence and boldness he will get up and give him whatever he needs." · *Father, make me like the persistent friend so I continually seek you, in prayer, for my needs and the needs of others.*

Luke 11:9–10 (AMP) "So I say to you, ask and keep on asking, and it will be given to you; seek and keep on seeking, and you will find; knock and keep on knocking, and the door will be opened to you. For everyone who keeps on asking [persistently], receives; and he who keeps on seeking [persistently], finds; and to him who keeps on knocking [persistently], the door will be opened." · *I choose to ask, seek, and knock in prayer. I choose to keep on asking, keep on seeking, and keep on knocking until the Lord answers.*

Devotional Thoughts for Personal Journaling

1. Think about times and circumstances in which you have had great victories in prayer and those times when you've felt defeated and tended to give up in prayer. Does victory come under a certain set of circumstances? What are they? Do feelings of failure seem to come under particular circumstances? What are they? Write down the answers to these questions. Ask the Lord to remind you to persist in prayer.

2. If you struggle to have a regular victorious prayer life, consider having a Christian friend hold you accountable in this area. Make a list of potential accountability partners, if you don't have one yet, and then pray over whom to discuss this with.

15

REX'S JOURNEY

A Lesson in Loving Your Neighbor

"'You shall love the LORD your God with all your heart, with all your soul, with all your strength, and with all your mind,' and 'your neighbor as yourself.'" (Luke 10:27)

My husband was just leaving for an appointment when suddenly he came back inside our home. "The neighbor's dog is standing on our driveway behind my car," he said. I went outside to find Rex, our next-door neighbor's black Lab mix, standing there shaking and looking a bit confused. Rex is an older dog with greying fur around his black muzzle. He seemed bewildered and shaken.

I tried to coax Rex to go back into his yard, but he wasn't budging. He just stood there. It was then that I noticed an invisible fence collar around his neck. It dawned on me that he had broken through his electric fence and was afraid to go back home for fear of an electric shock. Patiently, I got one of our leashes, took his invisible fence collar off, threw it back into his yard, and gently led him up the neighbor's driveway and back onto his own front porch. There I found his dog bed, food, and water bowl.

I retrieved Rex's electric collar, put it back on him, and then rang the doorbell several times to explain to our neighbor. No one answered. Apparently, no one was home. Over the next hour or two, I checked on Rex several times. He was standing in front of his own garage, still shaking. I went out to make sure he wasn't leaving his yard. I also tried to lead him to his food, water, and bed. Finally, I texted some other neighbors to see if anyone had a phone number for Rex's owners, since they had only recently moved in and I didn't know them well.

I felt a compassion for old Rex that was most certainly from the Lord. I couldn't understand why he'd been left outside when no one was home, so I just kept checking on him that night. I noticed later that he had been taken inside.

Eventually, although I couldn't find a phone number, I found an e-mail address for my neighbor and wrote to let her know that Rex had wandered from his yard and perhaps the battery on his electric collar needed replacement. The neighbor graciously replied the next day, thanking me for watching over Rex.

Since Rex was a dear old dog who belonged to my new neighbors, I felt a responsibility for him. I was concerned that he could wander into the street and get hit by a car or lost.

Certainly, I thought that I would want my neighbor to watch over our dog if she ever wandered out of the yard. I feel that in watching over Rex, I was following the command of Jesus to love my neighbor. In Luke 10:27, Jesus had asked a lawyer about his reading of the Old Testament law, and he correctly summarized it that way. Jesus went on to share the parable of the good Samaritan, in which he commended the actions of a (typically) despised Samaritan man who took the time to help the victim of a robbery while the religious leaders were too busy and indifferent to help him. In that parable, Jesus clearly taught us that our faith must have corresponding actions of love. It won't always be easy or convenient, but when we love our neighbor, we are demonstrating God's love for them and hopefully drawing them closer to Him.

Helping Rex, the new neighbor's dog, on his journey home was a small way that I was able to love my neighbor. How about you? If you are praying and watching for opportunities, God will surely give you a chance to love your neighbor as yourself.

Personal Prayer

Lord, help me to be like the Good Samaritan and love my neighbor in ways that are tangible.

Focus Verses and Prayers of Faith

Luke 10:27 So he answered and said, "'You shall love the Lord your God with all your heart, with all your soul, with all your strength, and with all your mind,' and 'your neighbor as your-self.'" • *I choose to love God with all of my heart, soul, mind, and strength and to love my neighbor as myself.*

Romans 13:9 For the commandments, "You shall not commit adultery," "You shall not murder," "You shall not steal," "You shall not bear false witness," "You shall not covet," and if there is any other commandment, are all summed up in this saying, namely, "You shall love your neighbor as yourself." • *The Law and the Prophets can be summarized in the command to love God and love our neighbor. Lord, help me to do both, by your Spirit.*

Devotional Thoughts for Personal Journaling

Read Luke 10:25–37. Contemplate some ways you've demonstrated God's love in tangible ways in the past. Make notes in your journal about those times. Ask the Lord, in prayer, to give you more such opportunities. Then watch and see what happens. Journal the results.

16

FETCH!

A Lesson in Endurance

Men always ought to pray and not lose heart. (Luke 18:1)

Bandit is an Australian Cattle Dog who belongs to a friend of mine. He has bright eyes and a bristly coat, and he's full of energy. Every time I visit the farm where he lives, Bandit is ready for fun. One would naturally assume that a dog bred for herding cattle would follow you around, nipping at your heels, trying to direct your steps. No, not Bandit. He leaves that to his friend Sassy, the Australian Shepherd who lives on the same farm. When Sassy was a puppy, she was a real ankle biter, but not Bandit. Bandit is a different sort of cattle dog.

How's that? you might say. If I didn't know by looking at his black, gray, and white mottled fur and brown points, along with his upright black-tipped ears, I'd swear he was a Golden

Retriever. Bandit is a master at playing fetch. He will play fetch anytime, anywhere, for as long as someone will play with him. And he never gives up. Bandit is the most adept dog at playing fetch that I have ever met. As soon as anyone is available to play, Bandit finds the nearest ball or other dog toy, picks it up, and joyfully brings it to his target with expectation in his eyes. If he is unable to find a toy or sizable stick, Bandit will resort to a slipper or even a wood chip! He literally picks up any scrap of wood and bounces over, ready to play another endless game of fetch.

Bandit is a blast, and his endurance wears out all the people he plays with. Every human who's ever played fetch with Bandit quits before he does, and that is no exaggeration. I sometimes feel a twinge of guilt when I have to call it quits with Bandit. Poor fella, he just wants to keep playing! His endurance is incredible.

Bandit's endurance got me to thinking of Jesus' teaching on prayer. In the parable of the persistent widow found in Luke 18:1–8, Jesus taught believers that we "always ought to pray and not lose heart." He used the example of a widow who sought justice from an unjust judge. She eventually received justice because of her stubborn persistence. Jesus stated in verse 7, "And shall God not avenge His own elect who cry out day and night to Him, though He bears long with them?" He encouraged believers to keep praying and standing in faith. Like Bandit's untiring games of fetch, believers should keep on praying for God's will to be done on this earth, and in our own circumstances, as it is in heaven.

How about you? When you don't seem to receive an answer, do you lose your faith in God's ability or concern for your situation? If so, take your cue from Bandit's endurance, and don't quit praying or standing in faith for God's perfect answer.

Personal Prayer

Lord, help me to have endurance as I pray and seek your will to be done in my life. I need endurance to run the race of faith and to keep on praying. Help me, Lord. Amen.

Focus Verses and Prayers of Faith

Luke 18:1 Then He spoke a parable to them, that men always ought to pray and not lose heart. • *Lord, help me to pray and never give up. I choose to keep praying and not give up!*

Devotional Thoughts for Personal Journaling

Read and pray through Hebrews 11, followed by Hebrews 12:1. What does Hebrews 12:1 tell you about the race of faith? How can you apply it to your life of prayer and your everyday life?

17

THE COMFORTER
A Lesson in God's Comforting Care

"And I will ask the Father, and He will give you another Helper
(Comforter, Advocate, Intercessor—Counselor, Strengthener,
Standby), to be with you forever." (John 14:16 AMP)

When anyone at our house is feeling a bit under the
weather or just needs cheering up, we know where to
turn. It's Joy the Cavachon who cheers us up. Joy was born
and bred to sit on the lap of her human companions, and she
does it very well. She's always a great cuddler, but when one of
us is feeling bad, she really rises to the challenge.

When my older daughter had her wisdom teeth pulled
out, Joy stationed herself on the back of the couch for hours
each day, comforting Hannah after her surgery. She would
stay nearby watching over Hannah as she dozed and would
only leave to go outside or to eat a meal. Her watchful care

continued for several days. Joy was a faithful companion during the entire recovery. It was as if Joy knew that Hannah needed special attention, so she sat nearby to be there for her friend. Similarly, she stationed herself underneath my bed for two days when I was stricken with a case of food poisoning. Her soft doggy snores comforted me as they drifted up to my ears from under the bed. When I would wake up, she would jump up onto the bed to check to see how I was feeling. I like to think that God uses the comforting presence of our little dog to remind me of His comforting love and presence in my life.

When Jesus was anticipating His crucifixion and earthly departure, He began to explain to His disciples that, even though He would be leaving, He was not going to leave them alone. He said in John 14:16, "And I will ask the Father, and He will give you another Helper (Comforter, Advocate, Intercessor—Counselor, Strengthener, Standby), to be with you forever" (AMP). Although they couldn't have fully understood His words at the time, we can now look back through His Word and see that Jesus was describing the Holy Spirit whom He would send to the believers on Pentecost, after His ascension.

One aspect of the Holy Spirit's work in the life of the believer is as Comforter. The Holy Spirit brings His supernatural peace and comfort to the believer in times of need. He brings that peace that surpasses understanding when we need it or just an inner assurance that He is with us. Every time Joy springs up on to my lap, I am reminded of that comforting presence of the Holy Spirit that is available to me.

How about you? Do you need a reminder that the Holy Spirit is Comforter to the believer? If so, ask Jesus to send His comforting Holy Spirit afresh to you today.

Personal Prayer

Lord, help me to believe you are still sending the Holy Spirit as Comforter today. Help me to know the reality of your comforting presence in times of need.

Focus Verses and Prayers of Faith

John 14:16 (AMP) "And I will ask the Father, and He will give you another Helper (Comforter, Advocate, Intercessor— Counselor, Strengthener, Standby), to be with you forever." • *Lord, I thank you that the Holy Spirit is Comforter and that He will remain with me forever because of my faith in Jesus Christ.*

John 14:18 (AMP) "I will not leave you as orphans [comfortless, bereaved, and helpless]; I will come [back] to you." • *I am not left alone as an orphan; Jesus has sent the Holy Spirit to me.*

Devotional Thoughts for Personal Journaling

Read John 14 in more than one Bible version, if they are available to you. Focus on all of the ways Jesus describes the Holy Spirit. Make notes in your journal of the ways Jesus describes the characteristics of the Holy Spirit and what He is speaking to you through your reading of Scripture.

18

WAIT FOR THE MASTER'S VOICE
A Lesson in Obedience

"To him the doorkeeper opens, and the sheep hear his voice; and he calls his own sheep by name and leads them out." (John 10:3)

On a family vacation to Talkeetna, Alaska, I met two darling chocolate Labrador Retrievers. They were aptly named Tally and Keetna. They lived at the outdoor adventure shop that their owners ran. Tally and Keetna greeted all the tourist visitors that came to their shop. That's where I met them. Their wagging tails greeted me one early Sunday morning as I entered the shop during our Alaska vacation. I was up before my family and had taken the hotel shuttle through the rain to go to town to attend church. The drop-off spot was at Tally and Keetna's shop. Ducking in to avoid a drenching downpour, I was greeted by this happy pair.

I immediately bonded with their friendly owner as I asked

her about local church options. We chatted and had a great conversation, and she was only too happy to share her dogs' tricks with me. Besides the usual "sit," "stay," and "down," Tally and Keetna were experts at another great dog trick. Their owner joyfully broke a dog treat in half and had them sit side by side. These two dogs were mother and daughter and were like a perfectly matched pair. As they obediently sat, their owner balanced half a Milk-Bone on each of their snouts. "Wait," she commanded. Neither one of them moved an inch. They sat motionless, waiting for the command of their master before indulging in a delicious doggy treat.

I watched with delight as they sat patiently waiting. In the midst of the busy adventure shop, the Labs were the picture of patience and obedience. Then their opportunity for reward came. "Okay!" their master declared. Gulp! Each dog flipped her treat off of her snout and into her wide-open mouth. It was as if those dogs were grinning ear to ear as they happily chomped down their treats. Everyone in the shop, myself included, broke into a chorus of "Good dogs!" in unison. What fun!

Tally and Keetna had been trained to wait for and listen to the command of their master's voice before they ate their treats. I'm sure that they had plenty of training and prematurely eaten Milk-Bones in the process. Like the two well-trained chocolate Labs, Christians can be trained to wait patiently for their Master Jesus' commands. Jesus promised in John 10 that believers would be able to hear and follow His voice. He said it this way in verse 4: "The sheep follow him, for they know his voice." In those verses, Jesus likened Himself to a good shepherd and the believer to sheep. Like sheep who are familiar with and follow their shepherd, so it is with the well-trained Christian. He used this word picture to explain what the Holy Spirit's leadership for the believer would be like. He further explained that the believer would be able to become sensitive to His voice and learn to follow Him instead of the voice of the evil one. Knowing and following the Master's commands is a promise to all believers.

In the flesh, I tend toward impatience and running ahead of God. How about you? Do you struggle with having enough patience to wait on God's answers to your prayers? With the help of the Holy Spirit, we can train ourselves to sit quietly, in prayer, and listen for His leading. When His specific commands or promises come, it will be a blessing to obey, and we will surely see the reward of our obedience.

Personal Prayer

Lord, help me to quiet myself and listen for your voice and your leading each day. Forgive me for those times that I have been disobedient and rushed ahead of you. Help me to train myself, with your Holy Spirit's help, to hear and obey your voice. Amen.

Focus Verses and Prayers of Faith

1 Kings 19:12 And after the earthquake a fire, but the LORD was not in the fire; and after the fire a still small voice. •

Father, I thank you for your Holy Spirit's leading that comes through His still, small voice.

John 10:1–5 (AMP) I assure you and most solemnly say to you, he who does not enter by the door into the sheepfold, but climbs up from some other place [on the stone wall], that one is a thief and a robber. But he who enters by the door is the shepherd of the sheep [the protector and provider]. The doorkeeper opens [the gate] for this man, and the sheep hear his voice and pay attention to it. And [knowing that they listen] he calls his own sheep by name and leads them out [to pasture]. When he has brought all his own sheep outside, he walks on ahead of them, and the sheep follow him because they know his voice and recognize his call. They will never follow a stranger, but will run away from him, because they do not know the voice of strangers. • *Lord, I want to be one that follows your voice. Help me to learn to be sensitive to your voice. I thank you now that through my faith in Jesus Christ I am sensitive to your leading.*

Devotional Thoughts for Personal Journaling

Study 1 Kings 19:9–12 and the surrounding context. What situation was Elijah in when he heard from the Lord? Was it a set of circumstances in which he expected to hear from God? Was it the way that you would normally expect to hear from God? Contemplate the message Elijah received in the midst of those circumstances, and let that message minister to you about your own challenging situation. Write down insights the Lord gives you from this passage.

19

DON'T JUDGE A BOOK BY ITS COVER

A Lesson in Looking Past Appearances

"For the LORD does not see as man sees; for man looks at the outward appearance, but the Lord looks at the heart." (1 Samuel 16:7)

It was a gorgeous late summer's day, the weekend before my oldest daughter started college. We had driven to one of our favorite places. It was an out-of-the-way beach on Lake Michigan, off the beaten track from the usual horde of tourists. The water sparkled in the sunlight, and the white sand warmed our feet as we savored one last trip to the beach. Our little dog Joy kept us laughing as she gleefully jumped in the waves. In spite of her small size, she attacked each new wave with a ferocity one might expect of a much larger dog.

A few others came and went that afternoon, and some brought their big dogs for a swim. We were admiring a black Labrador and a chocolate Labrador as they leapt into the water off of the dock. Again and again these big dogs would leap off the end of the dock to retrieve their specially designed fetching dummies. The retrieving instinct had clearly been bred into these dogs. My daughter and I, both dog lovers, were enjoying the show from our beach chairs in the late summer sun.

Soon another family arrived with their tiny Yorkshire Terrier. This dog was so small it made our fourteen-pound Cavachon look big. That little Yorkie wouldn't have reached knee-high on those big retrievers. To our surprise, however, the owner pulled out a tiny version of the rubber hunting dummy (fetching toy) and began to throw it into Lake Michigan for that tiny dog to fetch. The Yorkie bounded over the waves to retrieve its beloved toy. Over and over again, this itty-bitty dog played a heroic game of fetch in and out of the big lake. We were shocked and found the whole thing very entertaining.

This tiny dog, who appeared to be a picture-perfect lap dog, weighed less than seven or eight pounds at the most. Nevertheless, this dog was mighty. It had a great retrieving instinct, or had been patiently trained to play fetch. How funny it was to watch this tiny dog fetch its toy over and over and over. This was something one would naturally expect of a large Labrador bred for its hunting prowess, but a Yorkshire Terrier? Really? We laughed out loud at the sight.

That unlikely Yorkie Retriever got me thinking about an

old saying: "You can't judge a book by its cover." That silky little terrier appeared to be nothing more than a wisp of fluff, but underneath the coiffed exterior lay the heart of a feisty retriever. The Scripture reminds us not to judge others based upon their external appearance. First Samuel 16:7 says, "For man looks at the outward appearance, but the LORD looks at the heart." Sometimes I have to remind myself not to be too quick to evaluate other people based upon external factors such as race, age, clothing, social status, etc. Instead, I remind myself that God cares more about the heart than the exterior of a person. How about you? The next time you are tempted to judge a person based upon their external appearance, remember the unlikely Yorkie Retriever. It will make you smile and help you to see others as God sees them.

Personal Prayer

Lord, forgive me for judging people by external factors. Help me instead to appreciate their heart, the way you do.

Focus Verses and Prayers of Faith

1 Samuel 16:7 (AMP) But the LORD said to Samuel, "Do not look at his appearance or at the height of his stature, because I have rejected him. For the LORD sees not as man sees; for man looks at the outward appearance, but the LORD looks at the heart." • *Lord, I declare that I will see others through your eyes rather than my own. Help me to do just that. Amen.*

Leviticus 19:14–16 (AMP) "You shall not curse a deaf man nor put a stumbling block before the blind, but you shall fear your God [with profound reverence]; I am the Lord. You shall not do injustice in judgment; you shall not be partial to the poor nor show a preference for the great, but judge your neighbor fairly. You shall not go around as a gossip among your people, and you are not to act against the life of your neighbor [with slander or false testimony]; I am the Lord." • *I pray for your eyes to see into the heart of a person rather than judging by external appearances. Help me to have discernment from the Holy Spirit rather than issuing judgments according to the flesh.*

Matthew 15:8–9 "'These people draw near to Me with their mouth, and honor Me with their lips, but their heart is far from Me. And in vain they worship Me, teaching as doctrines the commandments of men.'" • *Lord, help me to draw near to you in my heart. Show me any hypocrisy in myself so I can repent and be cleansed.*

Devotional Thoughts for Personal Journaling

1. Have you ever felt that you've been judged based upon your external appearance? How did that make you feel? Ask the Lord to help you to forgive those who may have hurt you in this way.

2. Ask the Lord to show you if you need to repent of judging yourself or others unfairly based upon external factors rather than their character or personal integrity. Ask Him for any needed forgiveness and for healing in this area of your life.

20

EQUIPPED TO FISH
A Lesson in Spiritual Training

He said to them, "Follow Me, and I will make you fishers of men." (Matthew 4:19)

Our Portuguese Water Dog, Kona, was full of life. She had a zest for living unmatched by most dogs. Kona loved to take long walks and, in fact, needed them to decrease her excess energy levels. The Land of 10,000 Lakes (our home state of Minnesota, USA) was the ideal environment for Kona, who loved to swim. Our suburban home, however, was not, but that's another story.

Portuguese Water Dogs, as the name implies, are excellent swimmers. Word has it they were trained to leap off their owner's boat to help drag heavy fishing nets full of fish back to the boat. Their large webbed paws are perfect paddles, and their dense coats make them ideal swimmers.

I hadn't researched much about the breed when I bought Kona (big mistake). I just wanted a cute, nonshedding mid-sized dog, and she fit the bill. She was all of the above. In addition to her adorable self, however, she was an Olympic-caliber swimmer who was bred to do a job. One day as we took our usual walk past a local pond, she virtually begged me to allow her to swim. So I gave in. Off she ran into the water and promptly disappeared! *What happened to Kona?* I wondered. *Where did she go?* She had completely submerged herself in the water! Unlike the more familiar Labrador Retriever, which swims with the proverbial doggy paddle, keeping its head above the water and hunting prey in its mouth, Kona swam like a fish or dolphin with her head and body completely submerged. I was shocked! I'd been around dogs all of my life and had never seen anything like it! Eventually she'd pop back up for a breath, only to disappear again. I was dumbfounded.

We certainly enjoyed our walks and swims during the warmer months, and I never quite got over how funny it was to see my dog dive. I later learned that Porties have the unique ability to close their nostrils under water, which helps them dive deeply enough to go after nets. Who knew? Kona was clearly equipped to fish, and she needed a boat and a Portuguese fisherman too! She was perfectly equipped for her job, no doubt through years of careful selective breeding.

Kona's unique fishing equipment—her webbed paws, closing nostrils, dense coat, and submersible swimming skills—got me thinking about Jesus' call to some fishermen. The story is found in Matthew 4:18–22.

> And Jesus, walking by the Sea of Galilee, saw two brothers, Simon called Peter, and Andrew his brother, casting a net into the sea; for they were fishermen. Then He said to them, "Follow Me, and I will make you fishers of men." They immediately left their nets and followed Him. Going on from there, He saw two other brothers, James the son of Zebedee, and John his brother, in the boat with Zebedee their father, mending their nets. He called them, and immediately they left the boat and their father, and followed Him.

These four burly fishermen went from hauling in nets of slippery fish to a life of spiritual fishing with Jesus. They walked and ate and lived with Jesus, watching him share the good news of the gospel for the next three years. They watched him pray for and heal the sick and defy the laws of nature through miracles. Through walking with Jesus, they were equipped to fish for souls.

In the same way, men and women today can learn from the Holy Spirit and more spiritually mature Christian leaders to fish for people. Like the first disciples, we can be equipped to share the good news about Jesus and pray for the sick. Through reading God's Word, following godly mentors, and getting to know the Holy Spirit by spending time with Him, we can become well-equipped for spiritual fishing. Like Kona the Portuguese Water Dog was equipped for her job, Christians can be equipped to fish for the souls of people.

Personal Prayer

Lord, help me to pray, seek you, and get to know you better through your Holy Spirit. I pray for godly mentors who can train me to share my faith with others.

Focus Verses and Prayers of Faith

Ephesians 4:11–12 He Himself gave some to be apostles, some prophets, some evangelists, and some pastors and teachers, for the equipping of the saints for the work of ministry, for the edifying of the body of Christ. • *I believe you have given special gifts to believers to train the body of Christ. Lord, lead me to the best mentors and teachers so I can fulfill my calling.*

Matthew 4:19 He said to them, "Follow Me, and I will make you fishers of men." • *Help me to follow you, Lord, and become a spiritual fisher of people.*

Luke 5:9–11 For he and all who were with him were astonished at the catch of fish which they had taken; and so also were James and John, the sons of Zebedee, who were partners with Simon. And Jesus said to Simon, "Do not be afraid. From now on you will catch men." So when they had brought their boats to land, they forsook all and followed Him. • *God, help me to forsake all and follow you.*

Devotional Thoughts for Personal Journaling

Have you developed a plan to grow to spiritual maturing and learn to share your faith with others? If not, write down an action plan to help you grow into Christian maturity. Consider the following:

1. Do you read the Bible daily? Think of the best time to fit that in.
2. Do you have a mentor and accountability partners? If not, ask the Lord, in prayer, to provide them for you.
3. Can you increase your prayer life? Write down a plan to increase your prayer time each day.
4. Do you belong to a local church? If not, why not? Ask the Holy Spirit to lead you to the right church for you.

In these ways you, too, can become equipped to fish.

21

ADOPTED

A Lesson in Becoming
Part of God's Family

God has sent forth the Spirit of His Son into your hearts, crying out, "Abba, Father!" Therefore you are no longer a slave but a son, and if a son, then an heir of God through Christ. (Galatians 4:6–7)

Kona was full of untapped potential. In my suburban home with a family that didn't quite understand her high-energy ways and the possibilities if she were highly trained and disciplined, it just wasn't working out. I would train and give her a command, but Kona needed constant reinforcement from the whole family, which wasn't always forthcoming. Not everyone in my family was as passionate about dogs as myself! As a result, Kona was confused and just not reaching her potential. She was a working dog without a set of clearly defined job duties and a unified management team to direct her. Consequently, she was using all that energy and potential in destructive ways, such as getting into the garbage bin, standing on her hind legs to get food off of the counters, breaking through her invisible electric fence to chase the neighbors, digging holes in the yard with her paddle-like paws, and many more such antics. She also had a protective instinct toward me, and I had sensed she had the potential to bite if she didn't receive consistent discipline from our whole family. After some months, I prayerfully and regretfully decided that Kona should be re-homed with a family that understood her breed's potential and need for consistent discipline. It was heartbreaking for me, but I knew it was best for her to be adopted by another family.

I began to pray about this difficult decision. I knew she needed a place with people that understood her breed. I remembered a dear couple who owned two Portuguese Water Dogs and were excellent trainers. As God would have it, their daughter and son-in-law were on the lookout for another dog, and thus I was led to the perfect family. These folks already had a Porty who was being trained for search and rescue work. They were familiar with the high-energy ways of the breed and knew how to put these dogs to "work" so they would stay out of mischief.

Upon our first visit, Kona immediately ran in crazy circles with her new potential pack mate in the safety of their large fenced yard. She played in the special doggy sandbox especially designed for this breed's digging instinct and romped in their doggy swimming pool (a toddler pool especially set aside for the dogs). In spite of my pain, when Kona looked at me with a huge doggy grin on her face after digging a big hole in her new sandbox (and no one scolded her for it), I knew Kona was home. Her adoptive family has kept in touch with me, and Kona is now a fully integrated member of their household. She is being trained by an expert as a search and rescue dog to assist law enforcement. Kona was adopted into a family where she is loved, well cared for, and can truly reach her full potential.

Like Kona, who was adopted into a loving family that could train her and help her to fulfill her purpose, any person can be loved, accepted, and adopted into God's family. The key to any person's spiritual adoption is to trust Jesus as their Savior by faith. John 1:12 says, "But as many as received Him, to them He gave the right to become children of God, to those who believe in His name." The gospel writer John was talking about that kind of spiritual adoption that happens when a person puts their faith in Jesus, turns away from a life of sin, and becomes adopted as a child of God. From a place of security and love in God's family, any person can reach their God-given potential and fulfill their purpose in life.

Personal Prayer

God, I thank you for your gift of salvation through Jesus Christ. Help me to more fully understand the gift that I have received in Christ and to understand more each day that I am your child.

Focus Verses and Prayers of Faith

Romans 8:15–16 For you did not receive the spirit of bondage again to fear, but you received the Spirit of adoption by whom we cry out, "Abba, Father." The Spirit Himself bears witness with our spirit that we are children of God. • *Lord, help me to be free from fear and to receive your full love and acceptance as your child.*

Galatians 4:4–7 But when the fullness of the time had come, God sent forth His Son, born of a woman, born under the law, to redeem those who were under the law, that we might receive the adoption as sons. And because you are sons, God has sent forth the Spirit of His Son into your hearts, crying out, "Abba, Father!" Therefore you are no longer a slave but a son, and if a son, then an heir of God through Christ. • *I believe by faith that I am an adopted child of God and heir to God through Jesus Christ; therefore, by faith I am fully redeemed.*

Devotional Thoughts for Personal Journaling

Do you ever struggle with believing that you are truly adopted into God's family? Do you have issues with feeling God's love? Ask the Lord to show you, through prayer, why. Ask the Holy Spirit to bring to mind any people that you need to forgive, including yourself, as unforgiveness may be preventing you from truly accepting His love for you. Make a list of anyone who comes to mind and then choose to forgive others just as Jesus has forgiven you.

22

THE UNDERDOG

A Lesson in God's Acceptance

To the praise of the glory of His grace, by which He made us accepted in the Beloved. (Ephesians 1:6)

Beca and Tom had just come through a tough season, learning to manage their oldest daughter's chronic illness. Having reached a place of greater understanding of her needs and care, they were relieved but exhausted as a family. They all loved dogs and had recently lost one of their two beloved older pets. A puppy seemed the perfect solution in the life of this family. They needed to laugh and a new little furry face to cheer them up. They'd always had a habit of rescuing older dogs from the pound, but not this time. They knew God had a puppy for them.

And so the search for the perfect puppy began. Beca had grown up with Golden Retrievers and hers was a large dog family, so they all agreed to focus on that breed. With a specific time frame set on the family calendar, they located a breeder with a litter ready at about the right time. All of the male pups were spoken for, and only one little female remained. But there was a problem. She was far from perfect. In fact, she had only three legs. During her birth, the mother dog had accidentally bitten her leg off instead of her umbilical cord, and now the only Golden Retriever left in the litter was the three-legged girl that no one else wanted.

Would she walk normally? Would she require extra care? These questions swirled before them as they considered their decision. I should mention that Beca and Tom have a call to orphan care. They have two biological daughters and one adopted daughter, with the possibility of more adoptions in the future. So, to this particular family, the little three-legged pup was just the perfect puppy sent from God. She was just another little orphan, this time a furry one, to adopt. They embraced their new little pup with gusto and named her Georgia. She needed a little extra help navigating steps when she was young, but now she bounds up and down the stairs and plays at the dog park with all the other dogs just fine. Georgia loves every human she meets and embraces life as a dog who fully expects to be loved and accepted. She doesn't seem to notice that she's an underdog. She goes through life unaware of her imperfection, or disability, according to her owners. She's just one sweet, happy dog that has brought joy to her family. When other owners at the dog park express sympathy for her, she just wags and runs off to play.

Georgia greets me with a wagging tail every time I see her. She reminds me of where my focus needs to be as a child of God. I can focus on my inabilities and weaknesses, or I can go forward in my life focused on God's acceptance and abilities and choose to rely on Him. The Bible says in Isaiah 40:29, "He gives power to the weak, and to those who have no might He increases strength." Ephesians 1:6 says that in Christ we are "accepted in the Beloved." If I choose to remember that I am fully accepted and empowered by Christ, my attitude is much better and I accomplish much more for my family and for the kingdom of God. Jesus' love and acceptance help me to focus on His ability in spite of my own inabilities. How about you? Like Georgia, who knows that she is adopted and loved by her family, you and I can choose to believe that God loves, accepts, and empowers us. We can go forward in faith, allowing His love and strength to empower us. The next time you are tempted to focus on your inabilities, remember Georgia, the three-legged dog who doesn't even realize she's an underdog.

Personal Prayer

Lord, help me to focus on your strengths and abilities and not my own inabilities, weaknesses, and failures. I pray that you would empower me with your Spirit to live a happy, fulfilled life serving you.

Focus Verses and Prayers of Faith

Romans 1:7 To all who are in Rome, beloved of God, called to be saints: Grace to you and peace from God our Father and the Lord Jesus Christ. · *I choose to believe by faith that I am beloved of God, called to be a saint, and I can live in His grace and peace.*

Ephesians 1:4–6 Just as He chose us in Him before the foundation of the world, that we should be holy and without blame before Him in love, having predestined us to adoption as sons by Jesus Christ to Himself, according to the good pleasure of His will, to the praise of the glory of His grace, by which He made us accepted in the Beloved. · *By faith, I believe God's Word is true. Therefore, I believe I am chosen, I am holy and without blame before Him, I am adopted as His child, and I am accepted in the Beloved!*

Devotional Thoughts for Personal Journaling

1. Everyone has weaknesses and inabilities. Have you been tempted to focus on your weaknesses and sins? Ask the Lord to bring to mind any sin you need to confess or any personal weakness you have allowed to hold you back. On a separate piece of paper, write those things down. Now ask God, in prayer, to forgive you and ask His Holy Spirit to empower you to overcome that sin and get your mind off of that personal weakness. Now

throw the paper into the garbage can or burn it in a fire. Ask Him to help you receive His love, acceptance, and forgiveness and to change your focus to relying on His ability.

2. Have you struggled at times to feel God's love and acceptance? If so, use the above Bible verses and prayers of faith as memory verses and faith confessions for the next several days or weeks. Write them down on a note card and take them with you, asking God for a fresh revelation of God's total acceptance of you. There are no underdogs in Christ—only beloved sons and daughters.

23

RESCUED

A Lesson in the Power of Life over Death

"Most assuredly, I say to you, he who hears My word and believes in Him who sent Me has everlasting life, and shall not come into judgment, but has passed from death into life." (John 5:24)

Max is full of life. He is one happy dog. Max lives his life to the max. He belongs to my friends Abby and her dad, Bill. They rescued Max from a Humane Society shelter after searching several shelters for just the right family pet. They were looking for a mid-sized dog with a nice disposition. When Abby saw Max, she knew he was the one. Max is a terrier-pit bull mix who has grown into a mid-sized bundle of energy. He is a friendly guy who loves his family.

Although we don't like to think about it, if Abby's family hadn't adopted Max, he would ultimately have been euthanized as so many other dogs and cats are when they are not rescued. In other words, Max was on death row. His only hope was a stay of execution, which would only come if a family came to adopt him and take him home. Max was blessed and his life was spared when Abby came to the rescue. Now he lives in contentment with his family, plays in their fenced yard, and even cheers Abby on at her soccer games.

As I thought about Max's stay of execution, I couldn't help but think of my own. In legal jargon, when the governor of a state using the death penalty finds a legal reason to issue a "stay," it stops the death penalty from being carried out until further evidence can be introduced. If new evidence sheds light on the case, sometimes the defendant's sentence is commuted to life in prison. In rare cases, a full pardon is granted and the accused goes free. Similar to Max at the animal shelter, I was under a spiritual death penalty. Although I grew up in a family that attended church regularly and followed religious traditions and rituals, I was an unbeliever into my adult years. One night after a shocking brush with my own physical death, I opened the pages of my Bible and suddenly, in an instant, I went from certain spiritual death to new life in Christ. When I read Jesus' words in John 14:6 ("I am the way, the truth, and the life. No one comes to the Father except through Me."), it was instantaneous, as I was suddenly converted to faith in Jesus Christ. That was my moment of new birth as I believed in Jesus and came into new life in Him. I've never doubted the truth of God's Word since that moment, and I know that I will inherit eternal life in heaven when I die. The Bible says in Romans 6:23, "For the wages of sin is death, but the gift of God is eternal life in Christ Jesus our Lord." The penalty for my sin was certain eternal death and separation from God, but through His own sacrificial death on the cross, Jesus took the death penalty that I deserved. He died so I could be pardoned from the death penalty caused by my sin.

How about you? Have you been rescued from spiritual death and come into new life in Christ by faith? Your eternal life is as close as a simple, heartfelt prayer. Like Abby rescued Max, Jesus stands waiting to rescue you and bring you into the new life that He alone can give. If you haven't already done so, won't you say yes to Jesus today and let Him bring you home?

Personal Prayer

Lord, I thank you so much for the death penalty that Jesus took for me on the cross. I now accept (or reaffirm my previous acceptance of) that sacrifice in payment for my sin. Thank you for forgiving my sin, for the gift of life given through Jesus Christ and His death for me, and for the pardon and new life you've given me through Him.

Focus Verses and Prayers of Faith

Romans 6:23 For the wages of sin is death, but the gift of God is eternal life in Christ Jesus our Lord. • *Father, I thank you for eternal life that is available through faith in Jesus Christ. By faith, I receive Him and declare that I believe in Him.*

Revelation 3:20 "Behold, I stand at the door and knock. If anyone hears My voice and opens the door, I will come in to him and dine with him, and he with Me." · *Lord, help me to continually open the door to your presence and your will in my life.*

John 1:12 "But as many as received Him, to them He gave the right to become children of God, to those who believe in His name." · *Father, I thank you that as I have received you, by faith, I am a child of God.*

Devotional Thoughts for Personal Journaling

In your journal, make a list of loved ones, friends, and acquaintances who may not know Jesus, recognizing that without Christ, they are under a certain penalty of death. Ask the Holy Spirit to help you remember to pray for them on a regular basis. Use the above Bible verses to make personal prayers, inserting their name, for their salvation, e.g., *The wages of sin is death, but the gift of God is eternal life for* [insert name] *in Christ Jesus our Lord. Father, help* [insert name] *to recognize the need for a Savior and to accept your free gift of eternal life.* Keep this list and pray until each one is saved.

24

THROUGH THE VALLEY

A Lesson in Walking through Grief

Yea, though I walk through the valley of the shadow of death,
I will fear no evil; for You are with me; Your rod and Your staff,
they comfort me. (Psalm 23:4)

He was their first family dog, the only one their kids had grown up with. Gunner was the family's best friend. A Golden Retriever-Cocker Spaniel mix, Gunner was full of life and love. In fact, Gunner was truly a lover. He showed love to everyone who would allow him to. He'd just keep pushing until you'd let him love you. He loved playing with the kids and their friends most of all. Gunner was that kind of dog.

One dark day, Gunner wandered out of the yard of the hobby farm where he lived. He'd always stayed in the spacious country yard, but somehow he made it onto the rural road that ran nearby. Tragically, Gunner was hit by a car. The details of the accident were unclear. But, true to his loving self, he picked himself off of the lonely road and dragged himself home to the family he loved. Somehow he managed to live long enough to get home. The devastated family brought him immediately to the vet, but all hope for Gunner was gone. They were all together with Gunner as he was put to sleep to end his excruciating pain. Silently they wept as their beloved boy left this life.

It was hard, Kristin said, harder than she'd ever thought it would be. Kristin was Gunner's human mom, and his loss left her empty. She hurt for herself, her husband, and for her kids. The grief just plain hurt. Many tears came. As a Christian, she prayed for God's help during this loss for her family. The Lord graciously reminded her of a book she'd only just received from a business client who happened to be a publisher. The book was about a man who'd lost his beloved doggy best friend, a yellow Lab named Ben. It was then that the healing began. She read the book and tears fell upon each page. There were many at first, then fewer and fewer. She began to be healed as she turned each page. As she shared the family's loss and requested prayer via social media, the Lord brought many kind and understanding words, which flowed back to her and her family. As she walked through the valley of grief and loss of this beloved family dog, the Lord showed her that dogs are a lot like Him. They love us unconditionally, and in return they simply want our companionship. God was faithful to bring such sweet revelation even during a time of grief. No doubt about it, her prayers and those of friends on her behalf were being answered.

Like Gunner's family, who went through the tragic loss of this beloved pet, we all face loss in this life. Jesus never promised that if we followed Him our lives would be easy or problem-free. In fact, He said quite the opposite. In John 16:33, Jesus said, "I have told you these things, so that in me you may have peace. In this world you will have trouble. But take heart! I have overcome the world" (NIV). The loss of a cherished pet, a loved one, or of a relationship that we've prayed would be restored can be the worst of times in our lives. In those times, we can reach out to friends and ask for prayer or seek God's comfort through reading the Psalms, found in the Old Testament. When the psalmists were troubled, they cried out to God, pouring their deepest grief, bitterness, and pain out on the page. In Psalm 23:4 we are reminded, "Even when I walk through the darkest valley, I will not be afraid, for you are close beside me. Your rod and your staff protect and comfort me" (NLT). When we are walking through the deep valley of grief of any kind, if we cry out to God, we can rest assured that He will walk through that valley with us and that He will bring us out.

How about you? If there is a loss you've endured, whether a beloved pet or any other, why don't you acknowledge that pain to Jesus in prayer, weep any unwept tears, and ask Him to walk you through the valley of grief and out the other side? He will be faithful to bring you through. You don't have to stay in the valley; let the Good Shepherd lead you out.

Personal Prayer

God, I need your help to walk through times of grief in this life. I pray that when those times come, you will be with me and help me to lean on you. Lord Jesus, walk me through.

Focus Verses and Prayers of Faith

Hosea 2:15 (TLB) There I will give back her vineyards to her and transform her Valley of Troubles into a Door of Hope. She will respond to me there, singing with joy as in days long ago in her youth after I had freed her from captivity in Egypt. • *God, I believe you will turn my valley of trouble into a door of hope.*

Psalm 31:9 (NIV) Be merciful to me, Lord, for I am in distress; my eyes grow weak with sorrow, my soul and body with grief. • *Lord, I pray that you would be merciful to me in times of grief and help me to extend that mercy to others who grieve.*

Devotional Thoughts for Personal Journaling

Have you buried a grief inside and not fully walked through the grief process? Spend some time with the Lord, in prayer, asking Him to show you any unhealed grief in your own heart. Ask Him to help you acknowledge the unhealed grief and to walk you through the valley of grief, in prayer. Journal any revelations you receive, then search the Psalms and meditate on applicable passages.

25

BEAUTY FOR ASHES
A Lesson in Hope after Loss

To give them beauty for ashes, the oil of joy for mourning,
the garment of praise for the spirit of heaviness. (Isaiah 61:3)

It was time and they all knew it. It had not been very long since Gunner's passing, but he was gone and wasn't coming back. This family had a dog-shaped hole in their hearts. The Lord had been faithful to bring them through the valley of the shadow of death, and now it was time for a new pup. They all knew it. What kind of puppy should they get? Gunner had been athletic, and this was a high-energy family. And so the search began.

After deciding a new puppy was what they needed, Kristin began an online search for puppies in the metropolitan area where they lived. As she prayed and searched for breeders online, she felt an inner prompting from the Holy Spirit to adjust her puppy search to breeders in another part of their state. The family had agreed to look for a Golden Retriever, and after adjusting her search, Kristin suddenly found a litter that would be ready in three to four days. Another sign that this was the right dog was that fact that the breeders were like-minded Christian people. Kristin and her family were able to bring their new puppy, Ruby, home only four days after the search had begun. Ruby is a purebred, reddish-colored Golden Retriever. She was born on one of the children's birthdays, in July, which was right around the time they had first brought Gunner home (see chapter 24). They named her for her color and the red stone that is the birthstone for the month of July. All these signs and coincidences just added up to the fact that Ruby was to be their next dog.

Ruby represents a second chance for her family after the tragic loss of Gunner to an accident. They feel that God is a God of second chances and that Ruby's wagging tail and kisses are helping to heal their broken hearts. Every time Ruby climbs onto the back of the couch to drape herself around someone's neck like a doggy scarf, it reminds Kristin that God brings beauty for ashes. The Bible says in Isaiah 61:2–3, that Jesus, the Messiah, would "comfort all who mourn" and bring "beauty for ashes, the oil of joy for mourning" and "the garment of praise for the spirit of heaviness." And so He does.

The praying Christian is not left in a state of grief forever. If we ask, in prayer, for the Lord's help to grieve our losses, He is sure to bring us through and to turn the ashes of life's losses into something beautiful. While Gunner could not be replaced, Ruby has made her family smile again. She pouts when she gets in trouble. She offers her paw to shake even before being asked, in hopes of getting to share some people food and those long walks. It all adds up to healing for her family. Ruby really turned out to be God's beauty after the ashes of one family's tragic loss.

Personal Prayer

Lord, I pray that you would bring beauty for the ashes of loss in my life. Help me to trust you to work all of the bad things together for good and bring restoration in my heart and my life.

Focus Verses and Prayers of Faith

Isaiah 61:1–3 "The Spirit of the LORD God is upon Me, because the LORD has anointed Me to preach good tidings to the poor; He has sent Me to heal the brokenhearted, to proclaim liberty to the captives, and the opening of the prison to those who are bound; to proclaim the acceptable year of the LORD, and the day of vengeance of our God; to comfort all who mourn, to console those who mourn in Zion, to give them beauty for ashes, the oil of joy for mourning, the garment of praise for the spirit of heaviness; that they may be called trees of righteousness, the planting of the LORD, that He may be glorified." · *I thank you, dear God, that you sent Jesus to heal my broken heart, to set me free where I am captive, to comfort* *me when I mourn, and to bring beauty for ashes in every area of my life. I pray that you would take any spiritual heaviness off me and bring me joy and praise instead.*

Luke 4:18 "The Spirit of the Lᴏʀᴅ is upon Me, because He has anointed Me to preach the gospel to the poor; He has sent Me to heal the brokenhearted, to proclaim liberty to the captives and recovery of sight to the blind, to set at liberty those who are oppressed." · *Jesus, thank you for coming to heal the brokenhearted. I pray that you would help me to pray for others who are suffering from a place of faith that knows you can and will bring healing in response to my prayers.*

Jeremiah 31:13 "For I will turn their mourning to joy, will comfort them, and make them rejoice rather than sorrow." · *Lord, I thank you that you will turn my mourning to joy, comfort me, and make me rejoice rather than sorrow.*

Devotional Thoughts for Personal Journaling

Spend some time in prayer asking the Lord to remind you of times in your life when God brought you through a time of grief into a time of happiness again. Write them down as a way to remind yourself that God truly brings beauty for ashes.

26

THE PRODIGAL PUP
A Lesson in Coming Home

"But when he came to himself, he said … 'I will arise and go to my father.'" (Luke 15:17–18)

He was gone. That's all. Nowhere to be found. Dexter had simply disappeared. *What am I going to do?* the dog sitter wondered. *Where could he be?* She grabbed a flashlight and searched the woodsy area near the home where she was dog sitting on the cold, dark, and rainy day Dexter vanished. To make a strange situation even more mysterious, some neighbors had brought Chelsea, Dexter's cousin, back home. Chelsea came home, but not Dexter.

Let me begin at the beginning. Dexter and Chelsea are cousins. Dog cousins, that is. Beagles, to be exact. They are black, brown, and white. I should say that Chelsea is the top dog. She's the bossy one, and Dexter is the happy-go-lucky cousin. She's serious and he's goofy. Dexter has long, floppy brown ears. This pair are quintessential scent hounds, born and bred. They'll follow any trail they can pick up. They have regular doggy conversations with a neighbor dog, too, barking and baying back and forth. They live with their human family in a pretty house on a cul-de-sac in a Midwestern American city.

Their owners had to travel south for a family wedding, so Dexter and Chelsea were left home alone with a visiting dog sitter. With their invisible dog fence, doggy door, full water bowls, and visits from their sitter several times each day, everything seemed perfectly in place. Blissfully unaware that anything was amiss, Chelsea's owners drove south toward Texas. Everything went smoothly for the first few days, then it all began to unravel. The story was recounted to me by Garrett, one of Dexter and Chelsea's owners. As near as he and his family can piece things together, here is how Dexter became a prodigal pup.

All was well at home until the third day, when a storm or blown fuse caused the electricity at Dexter and Chelsea's home to go out. That in turn caused the invisible dog fence to stop working, and off the pair went to visit their doggy neighbor or follow a trail. In a blinding rainstorm, they wandered onto a busy road near their home. A young motorcyclist speeding around the bend saw them and screeched to a stop. Chelsea darted out of harm's way, but Dexter was hit. Broken and wounded, he disappeared. A neighbor found Chelsea and brought her home to the distraught dog sitter, but Dexter was nowhere to be found. The sitter searched to no avail.

For two long days and nights, Dexter was out there somewhere alone. He must have been lying alone in the dark, cold woods. Finally, however, he was able to struggle back to his home. The sitter found him outside his doggy door muddy, wet, cold, and broken. His fur was caked with mud and a worm had attached itself to his dirty coat. Dexter had a chipped, dislocated hip bone, a broken leg, and a damaged muscle requiring surgical repair. He stayed at the vet for several days. He was battered and bruised, but Dexter came home. Now, a year later, he is as good as new and back to his usual antics with Chelsea.

Dexter's story reminded me of the parable of the prodigal son in Luke 15:11–31. Jesus often used simple illustrations from everyday life to teach deeper spiritual truths. The prodigal son is the story of two very different brothers. One was responsible and stayed at home helping his father. In contrast, the younger brother took his inheritance early, left home, and wasted his money on wild parties, addictions, and other sinful living. After his terrible choices continued, he found himself homeless, emotionally broken, and totally without resources. In desperation and repentance, the Prodigal Son returned to his father's house, asking for forgiveness. His father welcomed him home, totally forgiving his sin and restoring their relationship. While there are many things that can be said about this parable, the main point Jesus made is the simplest illustration of the gospel. All people are like the Prodigal Son—their sinful choices separate them from their loving heavenly Father God. If an unbeliever recognizes her own sin and turns away from it, sincerely asking God's forgiveness, He will welcome her into His family as the Prodigal Son's father did. When a sinner repents sincerely in his own heart, God's acceptance is total and complete.

Like the Prodigal Son in Jesus' parable, Dexter the dog found himself far from home. He was broken, wounded, and caked with mud. The Prodigal Son in Jesus' parable was far from home, serving swill to swine in a literal pigpen. While Dexter was just being a dog who wandered out of the yard when his fence broke, as people we sometimes choose to purposefully wander outside of God's protection through our bad choices, just like the Prodigal Son did. We make sinful choices that can lead us to despair and separation from God. Maybe we are addicted to a substance, wounded by the betrayal of a loved one, involved in sexual sin, or holding bitterness in our hearts over some past hurt. In our sin, we've turned our backs on God and walked outside the boundary lines of His protection. But if, like Dexter, we return "home" by putting our faith and trust in Jesus and confessing our sins to Him, God will welcome us into his family with open arms.

How about you? Have you or someone you love wandered far from God's home and into the deep, dark woods of habitual sin? Are you far away from God's loving care and kindness? You can pray today for yourself or your friend to turn away from sin and head for your heavenly home in your own heart. God will surely welcome you back, dress your wounds, and heal you.

Personal Prayer

Lord, I admit that I sometimes stray away from your loving care and kindness. Please send me an extra measure of grace today from your Holy Spirit to help me stay close to you, where I am safe.

Focus Verses and Prayers of Faith

Luke 15:5–6 "And when he has found it, he lays it on his shoulders, rejoicing. And when he comes home, he calls together his friends and neighbors, saying to them, 'Rejoice with me, for I have found my sheep which was lost!'" · *Lord, I believe that you rejoice when even one lost person comes home to you. Help me to pray for the lost, to lead the lost back to you, and to rejoice when they come to faith.*

Luke 15:20–22 "And he arose and came to his father. But when he was still a great way off, his father saw him and had compassion, and ran and fell on his neck and kissed him. And the son said to him, 'Father, I have sinned against heaven and in your sight, and am no longer worthy to be called your son.' But the father said to his servants, 'Bring out the best robe and put it on him, and put a ring on his hand and sandals on his feet.'" · *Thank you, God of mercy and forgiveness, for welcoming* *lost sinners back to yourself. I am grateful for the grace you have extended to me. Help me to extend it to others.*

Devotional Thoughts for Personal Journaling

1. Have you been in a difficult place where sinful choices have gotten the better of you? Or perhaps you suddenly realized you had wandered outside the boundaries of God's protection? How did you come back to the safety of His care? Journal about that time as a reminder of God's grace and mercy that has been extended to you.

2. Make a list in your journal of those you care about that are far from faith. Ask the Holy Spirit to remind you to pray for these people to come to Jesus. Ask the Lord to put Christians in their path wherever they go. Remember to make notes of any answers you receive. It will help you to keep on praying for the long haul.

27

🦴

THE THERAPIST
A Lesson in De-Stressing

Don't worry about anything; instead, pray about everything.
Tell God what you need, and thank him for all he has done.
(Philippians 4:6 NLT)

We had gone to the wrong terminal. In our morning flurry, we were all certain that the discount airline we'd recently bought last-minute, deeply discounted airline tickets for an impromptu, pre-Christmas trip to Florida on, was located in terminal 2 at the international airport. Within minutes, we realized we were wrong. It was now an hour and a half before our flight, and we needed to go to terminal 1, which was some distance away by car. Traffic was heavy. We needed a last minute ride to make it to our terminal, but our driver had already left. And once we made it to the correct terminal, we would have to go through security—again. Time was tight, to say the least.

The preceding autumn had been particularly fraught with stress. Long-standing difficulties in our lives only seemed to be getting worse and not better, in spite of all of our prayers. This vacation was supposed to be a relaxing, brief break from the stress at home for my daughters and me, and now this.

We quickly regrouped and made our way to the correct terminal. To make matters worse, we arrived to find a long security check-in line. I went to check our baggage, and the girls went to stand in line at security. After checking our bags, I couldn't find my daughters. They were old enough to be alone, but I couldn't figure out where they had gone! Then my younger daughter found me and explained that a man had come out of nowhere and escorted them to the airport employees' security check-in line, which was much, much shorter. The man then disappeared into the crowd. What a godsend that was! We quickly got through security with more than enough time to spare.

Needless to say, after the previous month's stress at home and all of the last-minute rush, I was uptight. The previous evening, I had been praying and thinking of simple, relaxing things that I could do for myself. I had decided it might be fun for me to take my little dog Joy to a therapy dog training class. Joy was a natural dog therapist anyway—she made everyone she met smile—but this would allow her to "officially" visit places that dogs can't normally go, to make other people smile. The thought had made me happy that night, something I sorely needed. I had even spent a few minutes the night before our flight looking on the web for dog therapy courses. I prayed about it and mused how much fun it would be to have my dog with me at my book signings, on the hospital visits that I volunteered for at my church, and the like.

It was then that I saw her. As we cleared airport security, there she was. A brown-and-white Springer Spaniel, with floppy ears, a wagging tail, and a red therapy-dog scarf tied around her neck. Right in the middle of the international airport terminal, there was a therapy dog! I had never noticed a therapy dog in an airport before. I made a beeline for the dog and her owner. It turned out that the dog's owner was a volunteer. She and her dog Mimi spent time helping stressed-out travelers relax. Mimi and her mom were just what Dr. Jesus had ordered for me that morning. I felt it was also an answer to my prayers about whether to take therapy dog classes. After a few quick pats on her doggy head, I ran to catch up with my kids.

Later, after grabbing a quick breakfast and reaching our gate, which was in a completely different part of the airport, there she was again. Mimi calmly strolled through the crowded airport corridor with her owner, and we had more time to pet and praise this friendly pooch. This time, I was able to ask her owner about options for therapy dog training courses, and I got some great information. What a blessing. God had heard the desires of my heart, uttered in prayer the previous evening, and had quickly sent Mimi and her owner to the airport the next morning as a clear answer to my prayer.

It was also a blessing for my anxious heart. I took it as a small sign that God was with me, and that no matter what the coming days would hold after the brief vacation, there would be something fun for my dog and me to look forward to at our therapy dog training classes. I didn't need to worry. He cared enough to send a doggy therapist to the airport, after all.

How about you? Stressed? Distressed? Are you seeking some relief from the swirling tension in your life? Take a cue from my experience. Pray to God and find a four-footed therapist to pet. You are sure to find relief!

Personal Prayer

Lord, help me to look to you in times of anxiety and stress. Help me to bring my burdens to you and leave them. Amen.

Focus Verses and Prayers of Faith

Philippians 4:6–7 (NLT) Don't worry about anything; instead, pray about everything. Tell God what you need, and thank him for all he has done. Then you will experience God's peace, which exceeds anything we can understand. His peace will guard your hearts and minds as you live in Christ Jesus. *I am not worried about anything; instead, I am choosing to pray about everything. Lord, I bring my concerns about [share your personal concerns with the Lord] to you now, and I ask you to help me know what to do. I thank you now that you will answer me.*

Jeremiah 33:3 "Call to Me, and I will answer you, and show you great and mighty things, which you do not know." • *I will pray to you, Lord, and you will answer me and reveal to me things I would not otherwise know. I thank you for that revelation now, in Jesus' name.*

Devotional Thoughts for Personal Journaling

1. Do you ever think God is too busy to care about the small things that concern you? That is something that so many people struggle with, but it's just not true, according to the Bible! The above verse in Philippians tells us to pray about everything! Make a list of the smallest things that concern you and then spend a few moments bringing them to the Lord in prayer. Believe that He has heard you and will surely answer. Make sure to keep a record of your answers too.

2. If you struggle with habitual worry, ask the Lord to show you some fun ways to relax and de-stress! He is sure to answer your prayer.

28

FLUFF THE PRICELESS PUP

A Lesson in Value

Are not two sparrows sold for a penny? Yet not one of them will fall to the ground outside your Father's care. And even the very hairs of your head are all numbered. So don't be afraid; you are worth more than many sparrows. (Matthew 10:29–31 NIV)

As they walked past, I couldn't help but notice they were a few steps ahead of their tiny dog. He seemed to shuffle behind them on his leash. We were vacationing in Florida, visiting relatives and chatting outside in the beautiful December sunshine, when there he was. Just a little wisp of a fellow, he slowly made his way behind his masters. I said a friendly hello, introduced myself, and asked the friendly couple if I could meet their dog. His name was Fluff. Here is what I learned. These two "snowbirds" were winter residents of

Florida who hailed from Boston, so Fluff had come with them to their winter home. He was thirteen years old. Each morning when they walked to the lake, they carried Fluff, a tiny mixed-breed dog who weighed eight pounds at most, in their arms. Then he did his best to make the trip home, trailing behind his masters on his little leash. His steps were slowed by his age, but he valiantly trekked on.

Fluff had the cutest doggy smile but was completely toothless in his elderly state. Fluff's mom and dad told me he could only eat soft dog food now. This broke my heart. I scooped Fluff up to show him to my children. We all agreed that darling little Fluff, with his toothless grin, was one of the sweetest dogs ever. And Fluff was valuable. Though weak with age and infirm, Fluff the smiling, toothless dog was priceless to his owners. He was their faithful friend, and they valued him in his aged state. Their compassion and care for Fluff got me to thinking about how God sees us.

In a day, age, and culture when worldly value is often placed upon us by our youthful vigor, good looks, or what we can contribute financially, Fluff the dog (and his compassionate owners) stood in stark contrast. He became a reminder to me that God values us all. Weak or strong, firm or infirm, young or old, all people have innate value and worth beyond human measure. The Bible clearly teaches that all people are created in the image of God and are precious in His sight. Our value comes because God created us in His likeness. Humanity, the Bible teaches, did not evolve from a prehistoric stew of mud or spring from an amphibian over eons, contrary to some schools of scientific thought. Very simply put, God the intelligent designer created humanity. He also created the animals for humans to steward and care for. In stark contrast to a society that devalues human life to the point of a willingness to euthanize the elderly or the infirm, stood the godly, compassionate care of two people for Fluff the aging, toothless little dog. Fluff was priceless to them. You and I are priceless to God.

How about you? Do you ever struggle with feeling less than valuable? Maybe your self-worth has taken a few hits. Perhaps people have treated you less well than they should have. If so, remember that the God who created you loves you very much. You are priceless to Him.

Personal Prayer

Lord, help me to know the value that I have in your sight more and more each day. Help me to value myself so that I will walk in holiness and with grace toward others each day, simply because I know that you love me and that I am priceless to you!

Focus Verses and Prayers of Faith

Genesis 1:26–28 (NIV) Then God said, "Let us make mankind in our image, in our likeness, so that they may rule over the fish in the sea and the birds in the sky, over the livestock and all the wild animals, and over all the creatures that move along the ground. So God created mankind in his own image, in the image of God he created them; male and female he created them.

God blessed them and said to them, "Be fruitful and increase in number; fill the earth and subdue it. Rule over the fish in the sea and the birds in the sky and over every living creature that moves on the ground." • *Lord, I thank you that I am made in your image and in your likeness. I thank you that you created me and that you have a purpose for my life.*

Matthew 6:26 (NIV) "Look at the birds of the air; they do not sow or reap or store away in barns, and yet your heavenly Father feeds them. Are you not much more valuable than they?" • *I am valuable to you, Lord; therefore, help me to value myself.*

1 Corinthians 6:20 (NIV) You were bought at a price. Therefore honor God with your bodies. • *My eternal life, faith, and freedom in Christ were bought at the high price of the blood of Christ. Thank you, dear God. Since you paid a high price for me, I thank you that I value myself as you value me.*

Devotional Thoughts for Personal Journaling

Do you ever struggle with feeling less than valuable? Read the above passages from Genesis and meditate upon them as a way to get deep down into your spirit how very valuable you are. Pray for the Lord to bring a deeper revelation of your value in Jesus Christ.

29

THE THREE AMIGOS

A Lesson in Being a Prisoner of Hope

Return to the stronghold, you prisoners of hope. Even today I declare that I will restore double to you. (Zechariah 9:12)

The three dogs looked at me from across the invisible fence barrier that separated us. Tails wagging, eyes bright, ears pricked, they waited in eager anticipation, hoping for a game of fetch. The smiling dogs spoke without uttering one *woof*. On their grinning faces was painted one word: hope. All three shared the same hopeful expectation that I would step across the invisible fence barrier and play fetch with them before I left their home, where I was visiting.

Now I should mention that these three never tire of playing fetch. Jax, Cooper, and Bandit, two Golden Retrievers and an Australian Shepherd, are a nonstop pack of energy. They live on a hobby farm where they have plenty of room to roam. However, in the house where they sleep, they are (wisely) restricted to one room. Whenever I stop for a visit, there they are, tails wagging, tongues lolling, always up for another game. It's hard to say no to these three happy friends. If I were ever to feel lonely or forlorn, they'd be on the top of my list of potential pals to cheer me up.

On my last visit, I brought several new toys for them. They were thrilled and tossed them in the air for a few minutes, then their eyes turned expectantly toward me. Hoping to play fetch, they just looked to me. Who could say no to this fun-loving crew? Indulgently, I tossed their toys over and over. What fun!

The hope painted on their doggy faces served as a reminder to me that there is always hope. When a Christian is enduring any of life's inevitable difficulties, hope in Christ is always sure. Life here has highs and lows, but the active presence of the Holy Spirit in our lives can remind us that we can hope in Christ, no matter our circumstance.

If our focus remains firm on the hope of glory that we have through faith in Jesus Christ, the troubles of this life cannot maintain a hold on our hearts and minds. Practicing the spiritual disciplines of daily Bible reading, prayer, and fellowship with other believers keeps our hope alive. We can pray and speak Bible verses about our hope in Christ and, in so doing, we can renew our own hope.

How about you? When hopelessness tries to take hold of your heart and mind, remember my three doggy friends. They are always looking hopefully forward to their next game of fetch.

We can keep our eyes on Jesus, and like them, maintain hopeful expectation for the good things He has in store for us. As we focus on Jesus, keeping our hope in Him, we can trust the Holy Spirit to encourage our hearts through His Word and prayer. If we actively look to God for His hope, we are sure to find it.

Personal Prayer

Lord, I admit that I sometimes allow hopelessness to hold me in its grip. I repent of focusing on negative circumstances and situations in my life. Instead, Lord, I pray that you would help me to discipline myself to keep my eyes and focus on you and the hope I have because of Jesus' sacrifice on the cross.

Focus Verses and Prayers of Faith

1 Peter 3:15 (NIV) But in your hearts revere Christ as Lord. Always be prepared to give an answer to everyone who asks you to give the reason for the hope that you have. But do this with gentleness and respect. · *I revere Christ as Lord. Therefore, Father, help me to always be prepared to give an answer to everyone who asks about the reason for my hope, with gentleness and respect.*

Hebrews 6:17–19 (NIV) Because God wanted to make the unchanging nature of his purpose very clear to the heirs of what was promised, he confirmed it with an oath. God did this so that, by two unchangeable things in which it is impossible for God to lie, we who have fled to take hold of the hope set before us may be greatly encouraged. We have this hope as an anchor for the soul, firm and secure. It enters the inner sanctuary behind the curtain. · *I hold on to the hope I have in Christ as the anchor for my soul.*

Romans 5:5 (NIV) And hope does not put us to shame, because God's love has been poured out into our hearts through the Holy Spirit, who has been given to us. · *Hope does not put me to shame because God's love has been poured out into my heart through the Holy Spirit, who has been given to me.*

Titus 1:1–3 (NIV) Paul, a servant of God and an apostle of Jesus Christ to further the faith of God's elect and their knowledge of the truth that leads to godliness—in the hope of eternal life, which God, who does not lie, promised before the beginning of time, and which now at his appointed season he has brought to light through the preaching entrusted to me by the command of God our Savior. · *I choose to walk in the knowledge of truth that leads to godliness—in the hope of eternal life.*

Devotional Thoughts for Personal Journaling

1. List at least six things that you are thankful for today, and then praise and thank God for them as a way of renewing your hope.

2. Ask the Holy Spirit, in prayer, to show you the circumstances and situations that can leave you feeling hopeless. Pray for revelation as to how you can cope with these situations and maintain your hope in Christ. Write down Hebrews 6:18 (above) and memorize it to remind yourself that Jesus Christ is the anchor for your soul.

30

THE MANGY MUTT

A Lesson in
Hope for the Hopeless

Be of good courage, and He shall strengthen your heart, all you who hope in the LORD. (Psalm 31:24)

Sassy was a survivor who had been to the brink and back. She came to my family in a rather unusual way when I was a child. We lived on a hobby farm with acreage and horses, and we always had a large Golden Retriever who freely roamed the property by day and lived in a kennel with an insulated doghouse in our barn by night. Sassy, however, was different. She was a small dog of questionable lineage. She had no pedigree to speak of. Sassy was a mix of something and something else. A shaggy black creature of about fifteen pounds or so, with short legs, floppy ears, and a long tail, Sassy was unique. She became a fixture at our house and lived a long life as the ever-present companion of successive larger purebreds on the farm.

Sassy came to live with us after my uncle found her wandering beside a rural road near his farm. They had a pregnant Golden Retriever at the time and couldn't care for an additional dog. I supposed they had tried to locate her owners, without success, but I don't recall. So Sassy was given to us. She was a cheerful little dog who trotted after her larger sandy-blonde companion by day and slept in the heated workshop in a little dog basket by night. We all loved Sassy. At one point, her owners were found, and she went back to them for a short time. It turned out she had belonged to a little disabled girl. We were heartbroken to return her to her owners, but we understood. Not long after she left us, however, she came back to our house to stay. Due to an upcoming move, her original owners decided she should live with us permanently. We were all overjoyed, especially my sister and me.

Through the lives of two successive Golden Retrievers and a yellow Labrador Retriever, Sassy remained at our home. She was a tough little dog. At one point, though, it looked as if we might lose her. My mother and older sister had noticed she seemed to be losing the hair around her eyes. It seemed strange that bald patches should appear on our canine friend. A visit to the veterinarian revealed she had a very serious form of mange, a condition for which there was no effective treatment back then. The vet sadly advised us not to give her the annual preventative immunizations that she was due to receive, because her case was nearly hopeless. He didn't want us to waste our money on shots for a dying dog. My sister and I were devastated. We were closer friends to little Sassy than our older brothers. She belonged to us girls, and we'd already lost her once. We just couldn't bear the thought of losing her for good. He gave it to us straight. The odds were against Sassy's recovery, but maybe, just maybe, there was a slim chance of survival. The vet gave us a medication that might possibly help, but it required careful, patient, long-term application if there was to be any hope for Sassy's survival.

Night after night, carefully and patiently, my mom and sister applied the medication to our little dog. First, my sister applied gel to Sassy's eyes to protect her eyesight from the effects of the mange medication. After that, the mange remedy was rubbed around her eyes. Day after day, week after week, this process continued. The patient sat still while one or the other of us held her for her treatments. Although her case was nearly hopeless according to our vet, suddenly things began to change. Hope sprang forth as we noticed tiny new hairs growing in the bare spots around her eyes. Slowly but surely, Sassy was nursed back to health and returned from the brink of death. What joy! She became the faithful little mutt on our farm throughout my elementary school, high school, and even into my college years.

The miraculous recovery of our little dog taught me about hope and the power of persistence. The vet had nearly given up, but we decided to fight for Sassy's life. She defied the odds and lived, due to the persevering care she received.

Sometimes in life we see people around us who seem to be beyond hope. Perhaps it's a hard-hearted family member for whom we've prayed for many years, but there is no change in his life. Maybe we have a friend who struggles with life-hampering addictions or other life-controlling habits. We are tempted to give up on her and quit praying. But with Jesus Christ in the equation, through our prayers, there is always hope.

The clearest example of that is found in Luke 23:39–43 There we find the story of Jesus' crucifixion. As He hung to die on the cross, two criminals hung next to Him, one on His right and one on His left. One of the men mocked and cursed Jesus to his face, refusing to believe in Him. The other man humbled himself, admitting his own sin, recognizing that Jesus was God's Son and asking Him for eternal life. Jesus immediately gave the hope of everlasting life to the man who had humbled himself. In an instant, he went from being a totally hopeless dying thief to a forgiven man on his way to heaven. A hard-hearted thief was suddenly changed when he cried out to Jesus.

The same can be true for each one of us. The hopelessness of any sinner can be extinguished by the total eternal hope of new life in Christ, in an instant. The dying thief didn't have days, weeks, or years to consider a decision for Jesus Christ; he had a few breaths left at most. Sassy, our little mutt, had a similar death sentence. Her hope came in the form of a medication lovingly and patiently administered by her family. The thief on the cross had hope that came with his dying breath through his own choice to repent of his sin and put his faith in Jesus. His death sentence was turned into an eternal life sentence. Everlasting hope came through faith in Jesus Christ.

How about you? Know any hopeless people or hopeless situations, or feel hopeless yourself? New hope is as a close as a prayer breathed in a whisper from a sincere heart into Jesus' listening ear.

Personal Prayer

God, I need your eyes to see beyond hopeless circumstances to have hope for the seemingly hopeless people in my life. Show me how to pray and what to say to bring hope to others in your name.

Focus Verses and Prayers of Faith

Romans 5:1–2 Therefore, having been justified by faith, we have peace with God through our Lord Jesus Christ, through whom also we have access by faith into this grace in which we stand, and rejoice in hope of the glory of God. · *I choose to rejoice in hope of the glory of God.*

Titus 1:2 In hope of eternal life which God, who cannot lie, promised before time began. · *I have hope in the eternal life which you promised before time began, dear God. Thank you for that hope.*

Hosea 2:15 "I will give her her vineyards from there, and the Valley of Achor as a door of hope; she shall sing there, as in the days of her youth, as in the day when she came up from the land of Egypt." • *Lord, help me to see the valley times in my life as doorways to hope.*

Colossians 1:27 To them God willed to make known what are the riches of the glory of this mystery among the Gentiles: which is Christ in you, the hope of glory. • *Praise God that Christ in me is the hope of glory!*

Devotional Thoughts for Personal Journaling

1. Do you have a hopeless person or situation in your life? If so, write it down in your journal. Ask the Lord how to administer the medicine of prayer to this situation, and to show you any actions you should take to help. Read the Bible and listen to the Holy Spirit's guidance for a time, whether it is an hour, days, or more, until you are sure you have an answer. Then write down the prayer strategy and action plan that you receive from the Lord.

31

THE LOST AND THE LEAST
A Lesson in Caring for the Poor

"Assuredly, I say to you, inasmuch as you did it to one of the least of these My brethren, you did it to Me." (Matthew 25:40)

The stray dog darted into the shadows of a nearby building off of the street where we walked. He was skittish, and as we followed behind, we noticed him join a group of compatriots huddled in the shade to avoid the relentless midday heat and beating sun. To my shock, I saw that half of his body had no fur. His mottled gray fur had been stripped bare, and his pink-and-gray spotted skin was totally exposed to the sun's rays. The bumps and protrusions from his ribs could be seen just below the surface of his skin. I encountered this emaciated dog as I walked with a group of missions team members some years back in the Dominican Republic. The sights and sounds were unfamiliar, and I was shocked by the presence of stray dogs everywhere. For an American, this was an unfamiliar sight to say the least.

Our team was conducting leadership training meetings and evangelistic outreaches in the DR, and we'd had an afternoon off to explore the town. As we walked the streets in a group, strays flitted in and out of the shadows and some simply lay on the roadside for an afternoon siesta. But this particular dog really touched my heart. Some disease, perhaps mange, had ravaged his body, rendering him nearly hairless. His jutting bones spoke of his hunger. The culture of a nation where stray dogs freely roamed the streets was so foreign, so unusual. We had been warned not to touch the roving packs of stray dogs due to the potential for rabies, so all I could do was watch him helplessly.

As we continued on our way, we sometimes had canine companions trotting behind us in the dust. Then we came to a boy. Like the stray dogs, he wandered the streets, seeming to belong to no one. He wore tattered clothes, no more than rags really. One of his legs was three times the normal size, swollen with some plague, parasite, or disease. One of his eyes was obviously diseased and most likely unseeing. He was the lowest of the low, a street beggar. My heart was wrenched inside. It was almost too much to bear to see this dear little boy in this condition. We had no purses or much money, having been warned not to carry them due to potential thievery. We stopped and made efforts to communicate with him through those on our team who spoke broken Spanish. We invited him to our public street meeting that evening, explaining that many local pastors, who may be able to offer help, would be there. We offered to pray for him right there on the street, which he gladly accepted. I offered him the few remaining pesos in my pocket and the only food I had, which was a half-eaten ice cream bar. This boy was the lowest and the least member of his society. He was so wounded, so broken, it was nearly beyond comprehension. We didn't see an instantaneous healing, but we trusted that our prayers were working and hoped that he would be among the thousands in the street crusades that night. I later searched the crowds, hoping to catch a glimpse of him. Many people received Christ as their Savior that evening, and many testified to their healing.

The depths of the poverty and need that we had observed that day have never left me. They changed me. The sickly stray dog and the boy in rags reminded me of the admonition of our Lord in Matthew 25:31–46. He taught in those passages about the judgment of the nations that will come. He emphasized that care for the poor, the lowest, and the least will be a criterion for His judgment, saying, "Then the righteous will answer Him, saying, 'Lord, when did we see You hungry and feed You, or thirsty and give You drink? When did we see You a stranger and take You in, or naked and clothe You? Or when did we see You sick, or in prison, and come to You?' And the King will answer and say to them, 'Assuredly, I say to you, inasmuch as you did it to one of the least of these My brethren, you did it to Me'" (Matthew 25:37–40). He later went on to emphasize that if we do not take care of the least among us when we have the ability to do so, likewise we are not caring for Him. Sobering words from the Lord about the call to care for the least among us. We must be mindful of the poor and those that the Lord puts in our path, the ones we can stop for, pray for, and help in practical ways.

How about you? Do you sometimes feel overwhelmed by the needs of others around you and just give up in despair? Don't do it. Instead, stop for those in need that are put in your path and do what you can. I couldn't take the stray dog home that day and I couldn't do very much for the beggar boy, but I did what I could. I stopped, I prayed, and I shared what I had, then we invited him to come to a place where he could receive more help. In short, I did what I could. If each of us does what we can, that's a great start. As we help the least of these, we'll be doing it unto the Lord.

Personal Prayer

Lord, I pray that you would open my heart and open my eyes to the needs of the poor that you place on the path of my everyday life. Help me to care, to be concerned, and to do what I can do for them. Amen.

Focus Verses and Prayers of Faith

Leviticus 25:35 "If one of your brethren becomes poor, and falls into poverty among you, then you shall help him, like a stranger or a sojourner, that he may live with you." • *Lord,* *show me how to care for the brother who becomes poor, according to your Word.*

Psalm 12:5 "For the oppression of the poor, for the sighing of the needy, now I will arise," says the LORD; "I will set him in the safety for which he yearns." • *God, set in safety those who are poor, and help me to be an instrument of your mercy toward them.*

Proverbs 22:9 He who has a generous eye will be blessed, for he gives of his bread to the poor. • *I pray for a generous eye to bless the poor and share my bread.*

Luke 14:12–14 Then He also said to him who invited Him, "When you give a dinner or a supper, do not ask your friends, your brothers, your relatives, nor rich neighbors, lest they also invite you back, and you be repaid. But when you give a feast, invite the poor, the maimed, the lame, the blind. And you will be blessed, because they cannot repay you; for you shall be repaid at the resurrection of the just." • *Father, help me to invite the ones no one else wants to help in my world.*

Devotional Thoughts for Personal Journaling

1. When we see the great needs around us, we can have two reactions. Do nothing or try to do everything and fail. Ask the Lord to help you come to a place of balance and change your heart to do what you can do for those He puts in your path. Take a thirty-day challenge to pray for divine

appointments to help the poor that you encounter in your everyday life. Write down what happens.

2. How did the above experience change you? Ask the Lord to expand your influence among the poor in your community. Journal any revelations you receive as to your calling and what the Lord might be speaking to your heart.

Concluding Thoughts and Prayers

It is my hope that *Dog Tales & Pup Parables* has helped you to grow in faith and grace. I pray that these simple stories from life with my beloved pets continue to remind you of the spiritual lessons they illustrate.

I would be remiss, however, if I didn't leave you with some very important final thoughts. Are you perhaps seeking assurance of your salvation? Are you a Christian who desires a deeper experience with the Lord and greater power to be a witness for Christ? If so, keep reading.

The Greatest Miracle Is Eternal Life through Jesus Christ

Recall, from my own faith testimony, that I spent years attending churches, but lacked a living faith in Jesus Christ. Without that personal faith, the Bible clearly states, I would have perished for all eternity, separated from God's forgiveness. Church attendance, good deeds, giving money to worthy causes or churches, or any other religious activity, cannot bring a person into eternal life after they die. Faith in Jesus Christ alone saves. There are not many ways to heaven; there is only one way. If you are not absolutely certain that you will go to heaven when you die, you can be certain. The Bible says so. The single most important decision people can make is to simply admit their own sinfulness and need for God. Asking His forgiveness and accepting the free gift of eternal life, through Jesus Christ, will bring anyone within the safety and protection of God's grace. It is so simple. Even some churchgoers can miss the simplicity of the gospel because of rote religious rituals and traditions, as I did for many years. Romans 10:9 says, "If you confess with your mouth the Lord Jesus and believe in your heart that God has raised Him from the dead, you will be saved."

Focus Verses on Salvation

John 3:3 Jesus answered and said to him, "Most assuredly, I say to you, unless one is born again, he cannot see the kingdom of God."

John 14:6 "I am the way, the truth, and the life. No one comes to the Father except through Me."

Romans 6:23 For the wages of sin is death, but the gift of God is eternal life in Christ Jesus our Lord.

If you are not certain of your own eternal salvation, but you would like to receive and be assured of Jesus Christ's forgiveness, simply pray a prayer like this with a sincere heart of faith.

Prayer for Salvation

God, I admit that I have done, said, or thought wrong things, which are sins against you. I believe that you sent Jesus Christ, your Son, as a sacrifice for my sin. I believe that He died on the cross, rose from the dead, ascended to heaven, and will one day return to judge my sins and the sins of the whole world. I confess that I am a sinner who needs forgiveness. I now choose to accept Jesus' death on the cross as full payment for my sin. Thank you for forgiving me and saving me. I pray these things in Jesus Christ's name. Amen.

The Bible teaches that you, as a new believer, should declare your faith to another believer as a way of confirming your faith. The greatest miracle that can ever happen to anyone is receiving eternal life through Jesus Christ.

The Power to Be a Witness for Jesus Christ through the Baptism of the Holy Spirit

If you are a Christian who desires to receive the power of the Holy Spirit to be a witness for Jesus Christ, below are thoughts and verses on that topic.

The Bible promises not only eternal life to all who believe, but Jesus also promised He would send us another helper, the Holy Spirit, to empower us for service to Him. The believer is first indwelt with the Holy Spirit at the time of sincere repentance and salvation given by God's grace, through faith.

In addition, the act of second grace referred to as the

baptism of the Holy Spirit empowers the believer to be a witness for Christ and serve Him. It is accompanied by other spiritual gifts given according to His will as part of that empowerment. The believer's part is to ask, in prayer, by faith. It is Jesus' job to answer the prayer according to His timing. Read and study these verses and the book of Acts on this subject, prior to your prayer, if the topic of the baptism of the Holy Spirit is not widely taught in your church tradition or is not otherwise familiar to you.

Focus Verses
on the Baptism of the Holy Spirit

John 14:15–18 "If you love Me, keep My commandments. And I will pray the Father, and He will give you another Helper, that He may abide with you forever—the Spirit of truth, whom the world cannot receive, because it neither sees Him nor knows Him; but you know Him, for He dwells with you and will be in you. I will not leave you orphans; I will come to you."

Acts 1:4–5 And being assembled together with them, He commanded them not to depart from Jerusalem, but to wait for the Promise of the Father, "which," He said, "you have heard from Me; for John truly baptized with water, but you shall be baptized with the Holy Spirit not many days from now."

Acts 1:8 "But you shall receive power when the Holy Spirit has come upon you; and you shall be witnesses to Me."

Acts 2:2–4 And suddenly there came a sound from heaven, as of a rushing mighty wind, and it filled the whole house where they were sitting. Then there appeared to them divided tongues, as of fire, and one sat upon each of them. And they were all filled with the Holy Spirit and began to speak with other tongues, as the Spirit gave them utterance.

Acts 8:14–17 Now when the apostles who were at Jerusalem heard that Samaria had received the word of God, they sent Peter and John to them, who, when they had come down, prayed for them that they might receive the Holy Spirit. For as yet He had fallen upon none of them. They had only been baptized in the name of the Lord Jesus. Then they laid hands on them, and they received the Holy Spirit.

Acts 19:5–6 When they heard this, they were baptized in the name of the Lord Jesus. And when Paul had laid hands on them, the Holy Spirit came upon them, and they spoke with tongues and prophesied.

Prayer for the Power to Be a Witness for Jesus Christ through the Baptism of the Holy Spirit

Father, I yield myself to a life of serving Jesus Christ. I further yield my mouth to you and ask you to pray through me, as your Holy Spirit gives me utterance. I ask you to fill me with your Holy Spirit and give me the power to be a witness for Christ in order to bring Him glory. Please send your Holy Spirit to baptize me now. Amen.

About the Author

Janet DeCaster Perrin is a Christian author and speaker residing in Minnesota, USA. Janet is a mom and a dog lover. She is passionate about encouraging others to pursue a relationship with Jesus Christ and to walk closely with Him on the road of everyday life. She has served as a women's pastor, Bible college adjunct faculty member, church and Christian school volunteer, and missions team member. She holds a BA from the University of Wisconsin-Madison, a JD from Emory University School of Law, and a Certificate of Biblical Studies from ACTS International Bible College and is licensed for Christian ministry. She is also the author of *God Speaks: The Guidance of the Holy Spirit in the Book of Acts and Today*, available online.

You can find her blog at asamaritanwomanspeaks.com and can contact her at asamaritanwomanspeaks@gmail.com.